Field Guide to
a School of Belonging

Other Books from Teaching Empathy Institute:

A Year of Belonging
2019 Nautilus Book Award Winner

Other Books by David Levine:

Teaching Empathy: A Blueprint for Caring, Compassion and Community

**Building Classroom Communities:
Strategies for developing a culture of caring**

The Peer Partners Handbook *with Jerry Kreitzer*

Music by David Levine:

Can You Hear Me? Listening to the Voices of Children
Parents' Choice Recommended Award Winner 2019

Dance of a Child's Dreams *with Jay Ungar & Molly Mason*
Parents' Choice Gold Award Winner 1993

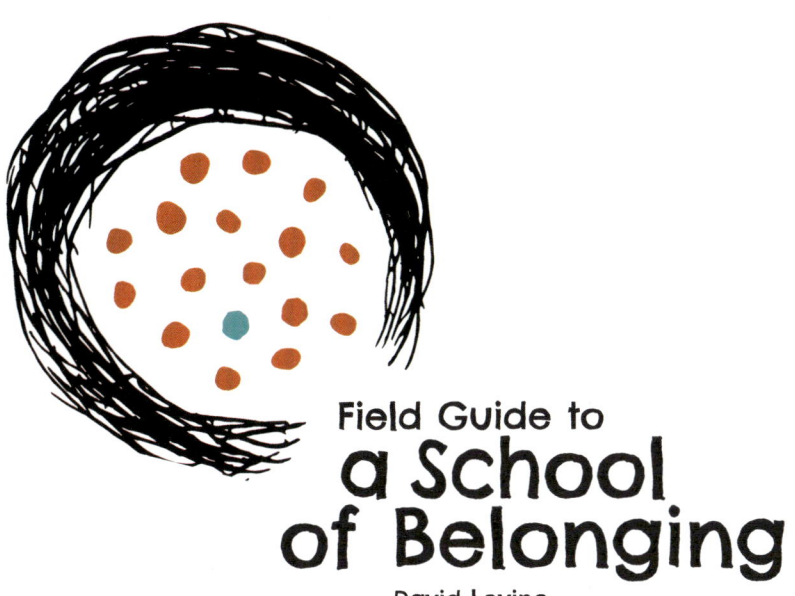

Field Guide to
a School of Belonging

David Levine
Teaching Empathy Institute

Teaching Empathy Press
PO Box 265
Stone Ridge, NY 12484
info@teachingempathyinstitute.org

©2020 by Teaching Empathy Institute
All Rights Reserved

No part of this publication may be reproduced, distributed, or transmitted in any form or by any means without the prior written permission of the publisher, except in the case of brief quotations and certain other noncommercial uses permitted by copyright law. For permission requests, please write to the publisher, addressed to "Attention: Permissions Coordinator" by either email or mail to the address above.

Cover design, text design & illustration by Sarah Burt
www.nographica.com

For details on acquiring additional copies of this book, please write to:
info@teachingempathyinstitute.org

ISBN 9781732776708

Library of Congress Control Number: 2018957962

Second printing May 2020

Printed in the United States of America

Visit our website at www.teachingempathyinstitute.org

Special thanks

to the educators in the Kingston City School District, in Kingston, NY, for their collaborative spirit and passionate work on behalf of their students.

Many of the social and emotional learning practices and processes presented within this Field Guide were inspired, developed, and utilized with the support of the Kingston learning community.

Table of Contents

Introduction 11

Chapter 1: Emotional Safety 15
    A Blueprint
    A Memorable Teacher
    Emotional Mapping
    Practice: The Community Meeting
    Process: The Inside Classroom
    Podcast: Emotional Safety

Chapter 2: Resilience 25
    Managing Life's Challenges
    Protective Factors
    Pro-Social Skills/Anti-Social Behaviors
    Social Skills Teaching Template
    Practice: Two by Ten
    Process: The Fishbowl
    Podcast: Resilience

Chapter 3: Empathy 41
    Emotional Memories
    A Story and A Song
    Shared Sorrow
    Practice: The Listening Wheel
    Process: Partner Guidelines
    Podcast: The Artistry of Empathy

Chapter 4: Reflective Practice 56
    Emotional Imprints
    Emotional Intelligence
    Feedback
    Dialogue
    Resonance
    Practice: The Check-in
    Process: Appreciative Inquiry
    Podcast: Emotional Imprinting

Afterword 69
    Podcast: Simplicity

References 73

Appendix 77

Materials related to the use of this book, links to podcasts, songs and classroom materials can be found at www.schoolofbelonging.org.

Teaching Empathy Institute

Teaching Empathy Institute

Teaching Empathy Institute (TEI) exists to promote the development of innovative social and emotional learning practices that meet the emotional needs of all students and the adults who work with them. Our hope is to build expertise through a "school within a school" focused on relationship building, social and emotional intelligence, and emotional safety as key components of a successful learning environment for students, school leadership, teachers, and other school staff members.

Purpose of the Field Guide

A Field Guide to a *School of Belonging* is our core resource, providing the rationale for TEI's baseline integration practices for designing and creating an emotionally safe learning community where every young person has a voice to tell his or her story and where every story has a place to be told. You can use this guide individually as a self-study course, with your colleagues as a book study, as a school-wide resource, or as a companion to TEI's digital learning resource: Fostering Empathy in our Schools and Communities.

Podcasts

At the close of each chapter, you will find a link to a short podcast by Field Guide author David Levine as a tool to reinforce the ideas and practices he presents in the chapter.

To learn more about our TEI digital learning tools, and other resources for teachers, principals, other school staff, youth workers, parents, and students, please visit our website: www.teachingempathyinstitute.org.

Introduction
Significant Adults in Significant Times

In 1984, I started my teaching career as a fourth-grade teacher at Woodstock Elementary School in Woodstock, New York, six weeks into a new school year. Due to overcrowding, two classes of twenty-seven students (fifty-four students total) were divided up into three classes of eighteen, and I was hired to teach the third class. Four months earlier, I had completed a master's degree/teaching certification program at Lesley University in Cambridge, Massachusetts, and here I was, in a new community in the Catskill Mountains of New York, as a classroom teacher on my own for the first time, in what I hoped would be a long career.

I couldn't wait to teach my own class, and yet, despite my enthusiasm, I also felt uncertain and insecure. I had never been a teacher with my own classroom, my name on the door, and my very own desk. This was all unfamiliar territory and it felt like I was putting on the identity cloak of someone else; it felt stiff and heavy. Up until that time in my young adult life, the only jobs I had held were musician, landscaper, summer preschool assistant, and health club receptionist.

On my first morning as a teacher, I arrived earlier than everyone. As I walked down the quiet hallway, a multitude of uncertainties swirling around in my mind, I suddenly stopped and stood there for a moment, whispering the following affirmation to myself: "I'm a professional." I took a deep breath, and said it again, a little more loudly. (I'm glad no one was around!)

Then, like magic, I was! I was a professional educator.

"My parents are going to be so proud," I thought. It was as if a switch had been turned on. I continued walking down the hallway to my classroom with pride and optimism, imagining that my footsteps were footsteps into what I hoped I would be in my career: a teacher who loved his job and helped his students succeed.

Since that moment on my first day in the hallway, my career has evolved in a way I never could have imagined, from classroom teacher, to social skills/empathy educator and trainer, to leadership coach, to professional development designer, to author, and now, founding director of the nonprofit Teaching Empathy Institute.

Since 1984, I've spoken with teachers in all kinds of settings in my various roles, and a central theme of our conversations has centered on how to best integrate social and emotional learning and community-building practices into one's teaching. I've come to believe that *before we seek to meet the emotional needs of students, we need to focus first on taking care of the emotional needs and competencies of the teachers* and other staff members in the students' lives.

Authentic communication, compassionate leadership, and relevant professional development are all pathways toward meeting a teacher's social and emotional learning needs. What does not meet their needs is to "templatize" the process by buying a new program with a binder and two-day training, with a mandate to implement the program in their classrooms. This all-too-familiar paradigm embeds a mental model that sounds something like:

> *This program is like one we did five years ago, only it has a different name. It will do until the next innovative*

Teaching Empathy Institute

approach, hot keynote speaker, or curriculum that will improve test scores as it improves one's self-esteem, comes along.

When school leaders seek to integrate social and emotional learning as a critical component of a school's culture, they enhance success through sensitivity and inclusivity. School staff need to be given the opportunity to have authentic and meaningful exploratory conversations with their colleagues as a *social and emotional learning (SEL) community of practice*. A *community of practice* refers to

> *people who share a concern, a set of problems, or a passion about a topic, and who deepen their knowledge and expertise in this area by interacting on an ongoing basis (p.4).*

Wenger, E., McDermott, R., Snyder, W. (2002). *Cultivating Communities of Practice*. Boston, MA: Harvard Business School Press.

Here are some reflective questions I have asked teachers to answer with their colleagues as part of the process of building an SEL community of practice:

- What is your greatest hope for your students?
- Who was a significant adult in your life?
- What is one of the nicest gifts you've ever received from a student?

Questions like these facilitate the manifestation of a phrase I heard once from teacher and author Marianne Williamson:

> *The further inward you travel,*
> *the further outward you travel.*

A Field Guide to a School of Belonging espouses the guiding principle that "the relationship is the intervention," and it takes the bundle of relationship skills that make up the empathic process, and uses them to help educators establish rapport and authentic connection with colleagues and students.

the relationship is the intervention

Most people who go into the profession of education care about young people, the community in which they live and, ultimately, about the future of the world. Youth are the future, and if we intentionally create the conditions of belonging, where each student has a place and each unique story has presence, then we will have continued the writing of our own story as significant adults in these significant times.

Teaching Empathy Institute

Chapter 1
Emotional Safety

> Honor is the capacity to confer respect to another individual. We become honorable when our capacities for respect are expressed and strengthened.
> —Angeles Arrien

A Blueprint

Often the idea of safety within a school conjures up images of single points of entry, name-tags, sign-in desks, and zero tolerance for fighting or other violent acts. These images focus solely on physical safety. In a *School of Belonging*, the articulation of a child's emotional needs provides us with a blueprint for emotional safety.

The four emotional needs are:

Belonging—Affiliation and attachment to the group and school community

Power—Competence; having one's gifts and sense of purpose identified

Freedom—Having voice, being listened to, feeling trusted, and offering ideas

Fun—Feeling excited, engaged, and joyful about discovery and learning

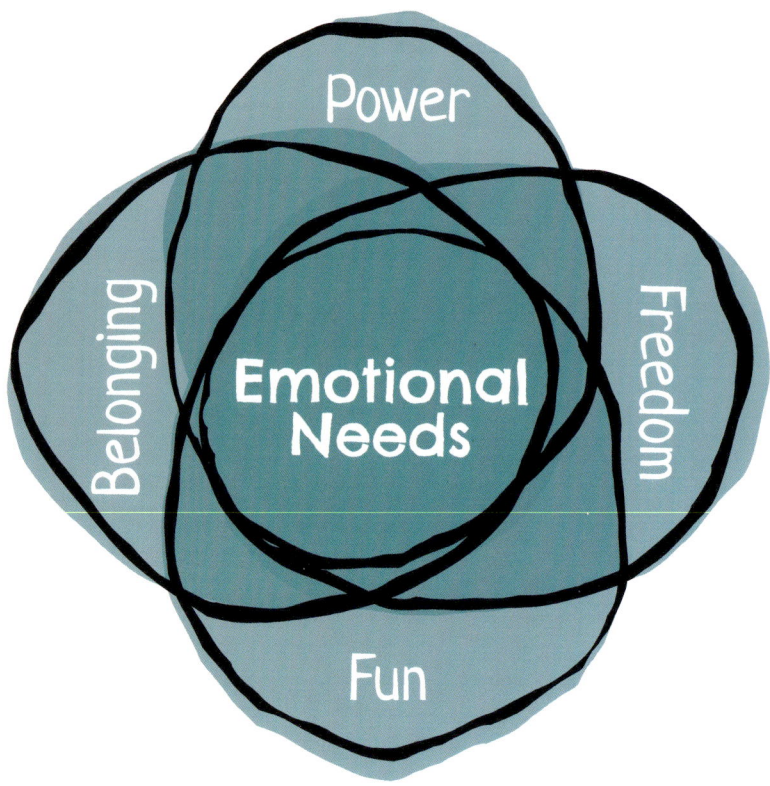

In a *School of Belonging*, there is a consciousness around creating a culture that is needs focused and non-coercive.

Needs-Seeking Behaviors and the Quality World

Behavior is a form of communication, and it is our challenge as educators to decode a student's behavior to understand how best to respond. Behavior is often motivated by seeking to get a physical or emotional need met. If, for example, you missed a meal, were in a learning situation, and suddenly realized how hungry you were, you would not be able to concentrate on the lesson (even if you were interested in what you were learning). Instead you would be fixated on the need to get something to eat. This is true for any physical need. If a need is unmet, it is difficult to be focused and present. That is why we feed our students breakfast and lunch if their families cannot afford to do so.

The same is true for an emotional need. When an emotional need is unmet, motivation will be low, often resulting in antisocial behaviors. If, on the other hand, emotional needs are met, this is what psychologist and educator Dr. William Glasser refers to as the "Quality School." *The Quality World* is defined as "the collection of pleasurable memories that we accumulate during our life" (Glasser, p. 58-59). A *School of Belonging* in its most effective form is a quality world experience, meaning that it is meeting the emotional needs of the students and staff; it is emotionally safe.

I once asked my colleague Karrel Greene who taught high school English in Sacramento, California, before she retired, how Dr. Glasser explained the Quality World to her. (He worked in her class while writing his book *The Quality School: Managing Students Without Coercion.*) Repeating what he did for her, she drew a happy face with a dot in the top region of the circle. She told me that each student has a point of connection, and our first goal should be to find that point and connect to it. This is what it means to establish rapport something all caring teachers and youth workers do naturally. This allows teachers to create memorable moments.

Glasser, W. (1990). *The Quality School: Managing students without coercion.* New York, NY: Harper Perennial.

My Memorable Person
  Mrs. Lopez: My Fifth Grade Teacher.

Description
  She was: Kind, Intense, Focused, Creative, Into nature.

  How I felt: Safe, Excited, Interested, Trusting, That she liked me.

A Memorable Educator

- Think of a memorable teacher, coach, or mentor from your childhood who had a positive impact on your life.
- How did you feel in that person's presence?
- How would you describe that person?

Teaching Empathy Institute

As you reflect on this memorable person, ask yourself how he or she has impacted your life today. The person you are thinking of is a *Quality World Person*. He or she met your needs, helping to create a positive and hopeful learning experience. This is a guiding principle of a *School of Belonging*—a place where the needs of all students are intentionally met.

What Do Students Need to Succeed?

As we near the close of this chapter on emotional safety, it is a good time to reflect on the students with whom you are currently working, or with whom you will be working soon. Ask yourself the question:

What do students need to succeed?

You might first want to articulate what *success* means, as this will help guide your answers.

Most responses will align to one of the four emotional needs: belonging, power, freedom, or fun. If you said, for example, that students need to feel a sense of achievement, that could be reframed as the need to feel like they have some power in their lives. By focusing on the four emotional needs, you can assess which pathway of response is the one best traveled.

Emotional Mapping

An Emotional Map provides you with a baseline from which to work as you and your colleagues assess the cause of a student's behavior. Utilizing the four emotional needs of belonging, power, freedom, and fun, the Emotional Map will assist you and your colleagues to efficiently and effectively identify an unmet need and an accompanying needs-based intervention strategy.

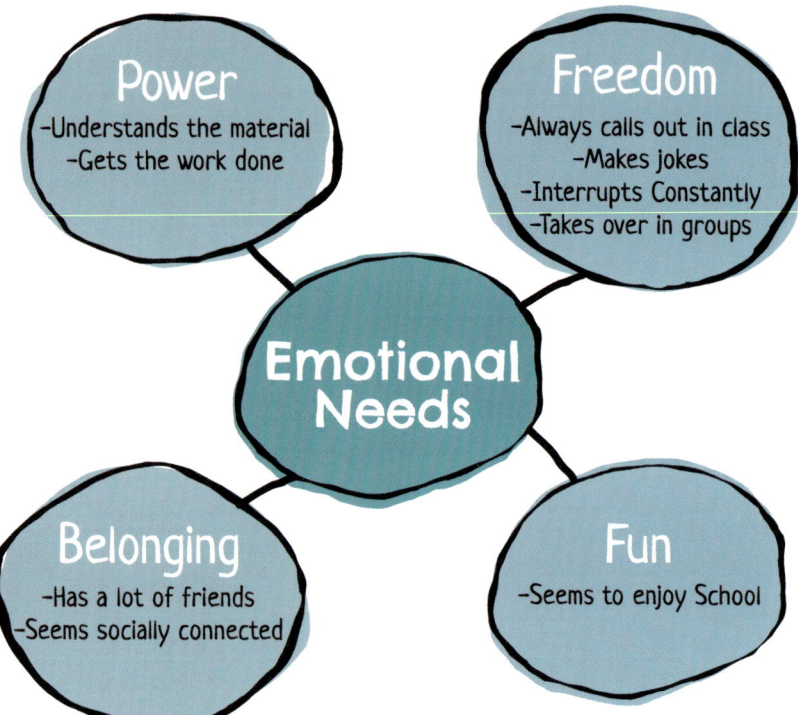

Here is an example of how the Emotional Map could be used:

1. To provide observations about a student as they relate to the four emotional needs (Be careful not to judge or label behaviors; just describe them.)

Teaching Empathy Institute

He often calls out in class

Makes jokes while I'm trying to teach the lesson

Interrupts me and other students

Takes over in groups and kids ask if they can be put into another group

2. To dialogue with colleagues or teammates to assess what your behavioral observations are telling you about this student and his or her needs

   It seems as if the need for freedom (defined as having a voice, being listened to, feeling trusted, and offering ideas), is not being met.

3. To create a management plan for the disruptive classroom behavior.

   This student needs to know that his answers are valued and that the teacher appreciates his presence in the classroom.

   The class needs to be taught how to work effectively in cooperative groups.

Working in this way provides you with a behavior-management plan while at the same time focusing on the student's unmet need, rather than on his or her personality challenges.

A Technique: The Community Meeting

What it is
A *community meeting* is an open forum in which students can share their thoughts, feelings, or ideas about a classroom topic or issue.

How it is used
A community meeting is used to set a tone within the group, practice social skills, and to gauge where the class is in relation to whatever issues are ongoing.

How to run one
Students are seated in a circle with the following guidelines:

- One person speaks at a time.
- No side conversations.
- Speak for "I" not "we," and state your name.
- Honor all views—do not judge them.

Once everyone is in place, present the rules and explain that a community meeting provides the class with the opportunity to talk about how things are going in the classroom. Everyone has the option of speaking but not all have to. It's a chance to speak and be listened to, and to understand where others (including the teacher) are coming from.

Once you explain the purpose and present the guidelines, you can open the meeting. There will be periods of silence and initially this will feel awkward, but it is part of the process. Let the community take care of itself; someone will eventually speak.

Teaching Empathy Institute

When you feel that the class is ready to move on, you can close the meeting and it will officially end.

Specific purposes:
- Prepares the class for a task at hand (a new lesson, a class project)
- Allows participants to give and receive feedback about work in process
- Allows class members to share concerns about something that has happened
- Helps students review learning
- Allows students to share positive outcomes from working together

Process

The Inside Classroom

The *Inside Classroom* is a contracting process that elicits and honors students' thoughts, feelings, and ideas.

Brainstorm with your students any or all of the following questions:

- What is it like to be chosen for a team at recess or in gym?
- What is it like not to be chosen or chosen last?
- What is it like to be invited to a friend's birthday party?
- What is it like not to be invited to a party?
- What is it like to be on the home team for athletic or academic competitions?
- What is it like to be on the visiting team?

Summarize their responses on the board, and then ask students to compare the two lists. Ask students where they would rather be and why. Then ask them to name specific guidelines for creating a classroom where everyone feels invited, chosen, at home, and "on the inside of the circle," rather than outside of the group.

Create a poster of the Inside Classroom guidelines and hang in a prominent place.

Podcast:
Emotional Safety: A Blueprint for Success

Listen at
schoolofbelonging.org

Teaching Empathy Institute

Chapter 2
Resilience

Help us to be the always hopeful
Gardeners of the Spirit
Who know that without darkness
Nothing comes to birth
As without light
Nothing flowers.

-May Sarton

Managing Life's Challenges

As youth travel on their journey through life, they will face both predictable and unpredictable situations that will be difficult. Often these situations deal with the unknown; entering kindergarten or moving into middle and high school are prime examples. It is in transitional periods like these that a young person's emotions are most vulnerable.

The challenge for educators who play a prominent role in the lives of children, is to predict what the difficult points will be and strategize how best to guide students in managing the multitude of difficult life situations. The other side of managing a situation is to simply cope.

To *cope* is to *deal with*, which is passive.

To *manage* is to *maneuver through*, which is active.

In this chapter, we will explore how to create the conditions for resilience as we teach the pro-social skills necessary for managing life's challenges.

The Comb Will Bend

If you were to take a comb (one of those small black ones), hold it on each end, and bend both sides down, you would feel tension from the center of the comb. If you then let each side go, the comb would spring back to its original form, and in doing so, it would be showing its resilience. That's what resilience is—to be able to spring back to one's original place even after a stressful event.

In her work on resiliency, human development professor and child psychologist Emmy E. Werner (1992) refers to protective factors. A *protective factor* is an "individual or environmental safeguard that enhances a youngster's ability to resist stressful life events and promotes adaptation and competence leading towards future success in life" (Garmezy, 1983, as cited in Bogenschneider, Small, & Riley, 1991, p. 2). Dr. Werner calls these successful people resilient because, despite the presence of multiple risk factors at an early age, they demonstrate the attributes of a person with "self-righting tendencies" (Werner & Smith, 1992, p. 202). They possess the capacity to spring back, rebound, successfully adapt in the face of adversity, and develop social competence, despite exposure to severe stress.

Literature on resilience often makes the point that when a teacher believes in a student, that teacher invites the student to believe in him or herself at a time when the student may feel that no one does. A *School of Belonging* is staffed with significant adults who consciously pave the way for their students' new life trajectories, who help students learn how they can believe in themselves and each other as they become equal members of the school and classroom culture.

Werner, E. E., & Smith, R.S. (1992). *Overcoming the Odds: High risk children from birth to adulthood.* Ithaca, NY: Cornell University Press.

> literature on resilience often makes the point that when a teacher believes in a student, that teacher invites the student to believe in him or herself at a time when the student may feel that no one does

Bogenschneider, K., Small, S., & Reily, D. (1991). *National Extension Youth at Risk: An ecological, risk-focused approach for addressing youth at-risk issues.* Chevy Chase, MD: National 4-H Center, Wisconsin Extension.

Teaching Empathy Institute

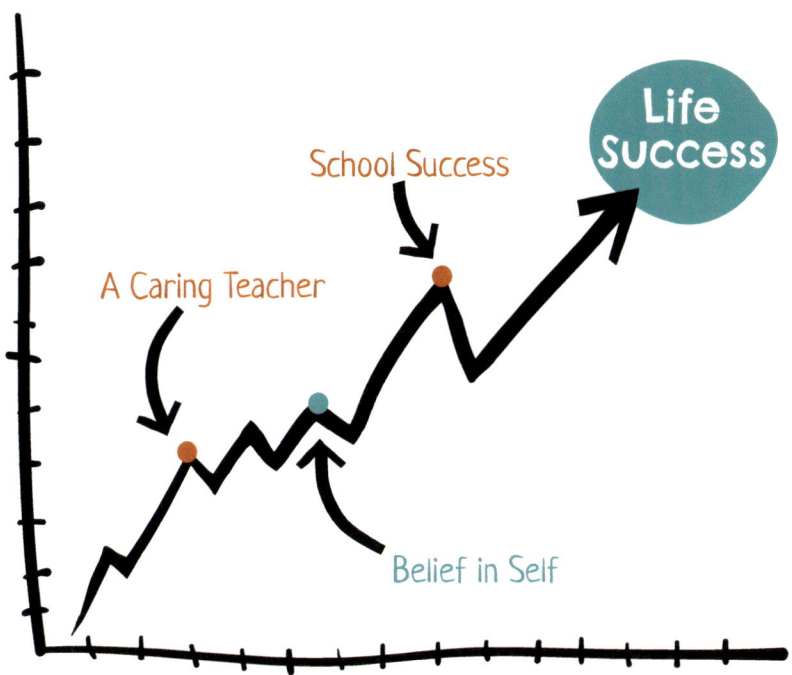

The life trajectory of a resilient student

Protective Factors

Dr. Werner also articulates that the more protective factors are present in a young person's life, the greater the chance for resilience. In simple terms, she describes a resilient young person as one who "worked well, loved well, played well, and expected well" (Werner & Smith, p. 192). Just as the blueprint for emotional safety is made up of the four emotional needs, the blueprint for resilience is made up of two types of protective factors: external and internal.

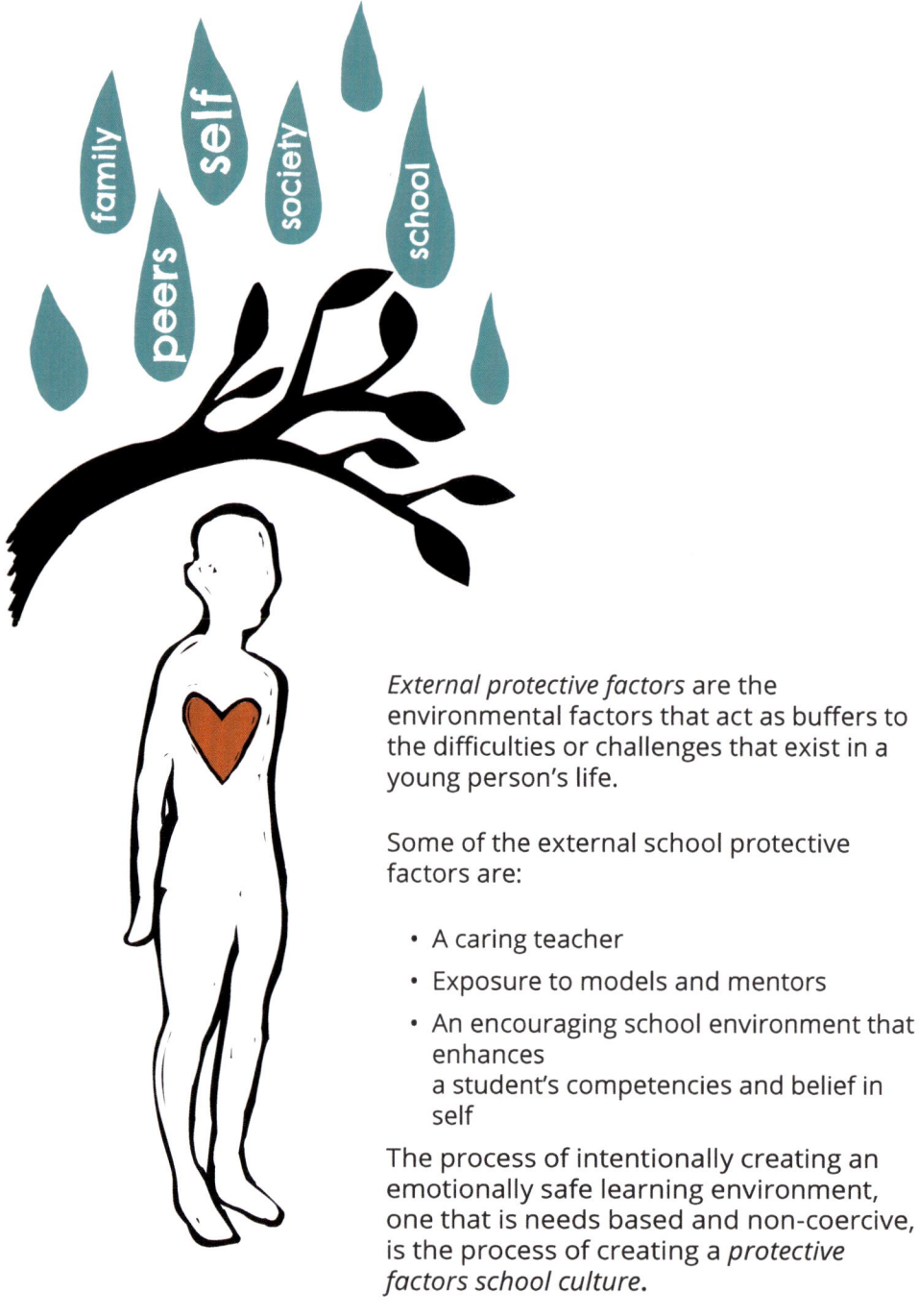

External protective factors are the environmental factors that act as buffers to the difficulties or challenges that exist in a young person's life.

Some of the external school protective factors are:

- A caring teacher
- Exposure to models and mentors
- An encouraging school environment that enhances a student's competencies and belief in self

The process of intentionally creating an emotionally safe learning environment, one that is needs based and non-coercive, is the process of creating a *protective factors school culture*.

Teaching Empathy Institute

Internal protective factors are self-regulating factors that can be summed up as:

Pro-Social Skills Development.

A socially competent student has the skill set to do such things as ask for help, join a game, invite others to play, work in small groups, act compassionately, and regulate his or her feelings. Dr. Werner (Werner & Smith, P. 202) refers to pro-social skills as the "great protectors."

Some additional internal protective factors are:

- Positive peer relationships
- A sense of independence
- A sense of purpose
- Participation and involvement
- School success

The presence of both external (environmental) and internal (self-regulating) protective factors helps create a sense of equilibrium in the life of a child.

Pro-Social Skills/Anti-Social Behaviors

In chapter one, I pointed out that behavior is a form of communication. When a student does not have the pro-social skills to manage a difficult life situation and is experiencing the stress of feeling less powerful than his or her peers, anti-social behaviors will arise, including bullying and other forms of low-level aggression. *Bullying* or *victimization* is defined as:

> *When a person is being exposed, repeatedly and over time, to negative actions on the part of one or more persons.*

Olweus, D. (1993). *Bullying at school: What we know and what we can do.* London: Wiley-Blackwell Publishing.

In a *School of Belonging*, behaviors are not labeled but addressed as forms of communication. Bullying and other low-level forms of aggression are dealt with therapeutically and with compassion through high-level listening in what is known as a strength-based intervention. A strength-based intervention utilizes the student as his or her own resource, trusting that with support, nonjudgmental listening, guidance, and practice, that person will learn how to better trust his or her moral compass and intuitive voice while in the throes of a difficult decision in a social situation.

Anti-Social Behaviors (Bullying)

Teaching Empathy Institute

Pro-Social Skills (Empathy)

To support young people in altering their anti-social behaviors, we must teach replacement behaviors. This will not only minimize bullying in school but also prepare young people to manage the challenges they will face in the future. These replacement behaviors could also be called high-level pro-social skills.

What do you think are the five most important pro-social skills to teach your students?

In a *School of Belonging* there are five primary pro-social skills embedded into the learning process.

1. **Listening:** Students are often told to listen, but not *how to* listen. As with any new skill, listening needs to be broken down into its various components. Each component must be presented, practiced, modeled, expected, and celebrated as it is demonstrated by the learner. A high-level listener maintains eye contact, is conscious of nonverbal responses, asks questions, and summarizes. A listener is focused on the other person. He or she does not talk about him- or herself, but instead provides nonverbal cues to indicate that he or she is present with the speaker.

2. **Empathy:** An operational definition of *empathy* is the ability to understand how another is feeling and then to act on what you perceive. There are numerous ways that educators can infuse empathy into their teaching and classroom culture. Here are some examples:

Teaching Empathy Institute

- **Literature:** Examine the various perspectives of the main characters in any story your class is studying.

- **Social studies:** Infuse the concept of empathic decision-making when it comes to examining how different groups of people are affected by governmental policy decisions.

- **History:** Highlight successful diplomatic efforts throughout world history that were enhanced by the empathic practices of listening non-judgmentally with understanding and compassion.

- **Resolving and mediating conflicts:** Apply conflict resolution to the daily relationships that exist between your students and teachers within the school community. Use empathic practices when intervening or mediating between two or more students who are in conflict or disagreement.

3. **Self-responsibility:** Responsibility can be presented as respond-ability: the ability to respond. Framed in this way, you can teach your students to devise a "response plan" for many of life's stressors, such as helping the family at home, studying for a test, following through on agreements, managing frustration, or doing homework. When responsibility is perceived as something a student has control over, it becomes more of a challenge than something he or she has to do.

4. **Solving disagreements with others:** Conflict is a natural part of life and something that students (and adults) do not always have the skills to manage. The combination of listening, empathy, and self-responsibility serve as the platform for conflict management. When students practice and recognize the need for conflict management, there will be a greater chance they work through their disagreements without needing an adult to do it for them.

5. **Goal-setting:** Goals need to be specific, real life, and reachable. Many goal-setting exercises, facilitated with the best of intentions, are general and unclear in their expectations. When a student articulates his or her short-term goals, this articulation clarifies his or her vision, providing a specific destination. I present goal-setting in the context of leaving a legacy. Through this lens, students see how their actions determine how people see them. Legacy provides a sense of purpose, helping to create meaningful goals.

Social Discovery

A few years ago, I was preparing to teach a social skills lesson to a group of seventh-grade students. I had my guitar with me, ready to facilitate a process I call *music dialogue*. As the students began arriving, this one brave girl came up to talk to me, and the following conversation took place:

> **Student:** Are you going to play that guitar?
>
> **Me:** Yes, I am.
>
> **Student:** Oh. Are you going to sing?
>
> **Me:** Yes, probably.
>
> **Student:** Not to be mean or nothing, but are you going to sing self-esteem sing-a-long, feel-good songs?
>
> **Me:** No, I won't be singing those kinds of songs.
>
> **Student:** Well, that's a relief!

As the student turned to walk away, I asked, with a smile on my face:

> **Me:** What kinds of songs should I sing?
>
> **Student:** You seem kind of nice, and I'm sure you mean well, but if you tell us about how we should act, how we should be nice and not be mean and stuff like that, we'll tune you out. We've been hearing stuff like that forever. You know?

Me: Okay. Yeah, I get it. But again, let me ask, what kinds of songs should I sing?

Student: Whatever you do, make it real life. Make it stuff we can relate to and don't lecture us about it.

Me: When we finish, let me know how I did.

At the end of our session, as the students were leaving, she looked over at me and gave me a thumbs up. I guess I did okay.

I never forgot that exchange, and I often begin my student sessions by saying, "Today we are going to have a lesson about real life." This usually gets many kids wondering, "What does that mean?" and away we go into what I refer to as a social discovery session.

Two highly effective approaches for teaching social discovery sessions that are real life are:

- Role-playing
- Modeling

Role-Playing

Role-playing engages students in dialogue, reflection, and demonstration and is often a favorite learning method of students. During a role-play, students are presented with a challenging real-life social situation that involves a decision, and they determine what the best pro-social choice would be. One example might be how to tell a classmate that you were invited to a party when you know your friend wasn't. This situation rings true and infuses the skills of empathy, listening, self-regulation, and assertiveness into the process.

What are some typically challenging social situations your students face daily?

The list that you create provides a roster of role-play scenarios to present to your students. The relevance of role-play is that it teaches students how often they know what is best for themselves and others, as they figure out their place in the social dynamic of the class, grade, or school. Three conditions of resilience grow out of role-play practice: self-confidence, perspective, and hope.

Modeling

Bandura, A. (1997). *Self-Efficacy: The Exercise of Control.* New York, NY: W.H. Freeman and Company.

The *Social Learning Theory* of Albert Bandura is a foundational theoretical component of a *School of Belonging*. Children do not learn their social behaviors through trial and error but through imitation. As a teacher, a successful practice in teaching pro-social skills is to model them yourself. If we want our students to be understanding, we must be understanding. If we want them to quiet down, we will not have much success if we yell at them to be quiet. Instead, in a quiet tone of voice, we could ask them to quiet down and explain why we need them to do so.

One critical application for social learning theory to low-level forms of aggression is to *avoid sarcasm* with your students. When a teacher is sarcastic, three things happen.

1. It teaches sarcasm as an appropriate way of communicating with another person.

2. It puts the student who is the target of the sarcasm on the spot.

3. It creates an unsafe classroom or group environment for the other students. A resilient young person is also a vulnerable young person, and we must always be mindful of how we interact with our students.

Teaching Empathy Institute

The core question we must ask ourselves is, *What kind of relationship do we want to build?* In the end, it all comes down to the wise words of teacher, author, and youth worker Martin Brokenleg who once said this:

"Programs don't fix kids, relationships do."

Brokenleg, M., personal communication, (2004)

Following is a template to help you customize a social-skills learning experience for your students. Utilizing the knowledge and skills presented earlier in this book, design a simple social-skills lesson.

Social Skills Teaching Template

1. Skill:

2. Reason for choosing this skill:

3. Introducing the skill: What is your framing statement?

4. Modeling the skill: How will you model the skill for your class?

5. Presenting the guidelines for the skill and identifying what they are:

6. Assigning students to work in pairs to practice the skill.

7. Processing with the class: What questions will you ask?

8. Assigning homework: How will you have the students practice the skill at home?

Two by Ten

Select a student who is disconnected from the learning environment either socially or academically. For ten days in a row, provide that student with two minutes of uninterrupted one-on-one time. Make this a ritual, and you will notice a change in that student's behavior.

This is known as a *micro-interaction* in practice and is one of the most meaningful and attainable forms of building resilience. When adults in school are conscious of the littlest of moments, these micro-interactions can make a huge difference for the recipient. Young people remember specific events when there is an emotion or a strong feeling attached to that event. A micro-interaction is one of the most significant external protective factors because it shows that an adult in the school cares. It doesn't take a lot of time for the adult, but it means a lot to the student when micro-interactions are part of the norm of the school's culture.

A Technique: The Fishbowl

What it is.
A *fishbowl* is a communication process that helps develop students' pro-social skills.

How it is used.
A fishbowl is used to address a classroom issue or concern while integrating numerous pro-social skills.

How to run one.
Start out with the entire class seated in a circle. Run a community meeting (see page 22) focusing on a specific issue. After five to ten minutes, stop the meeting and invite six to eight volunteers to sit in a small circle inside the larger one. The inner circle participants are called the fish and the outer circle participants are called the bowl.

As the fish interact, the students in the outside of the circle (the bowl) observe, listen, and provide feedback at times you designate.

There are usually two rounds, meaning you provide an opening question such as, "Why do some students act out when there is a substitute teacher?" This opens round one, and after the fish have talked over this question for a few minutes, pause the fish and invite process feedback from the bowl. This feedback focuses on what was said, who said it, and what the tone or mood of the inner circle was.

After this feedback, a second round takes place with a follow-up question: "How can we make things better for a substitute if our teacher is ever out?" After a few minutes, stop the fish and invite additional feedback from the bowl.

Thank the fish and have them rejoin the circle where the class can now join in the conversation to close out the exercise.

Continued...

Specific Purposes

1. Resolving conflicts (the disputants become the fish)
2. Planning
3. Reviewing what has been learned
4. Exploring classroom issues
5. Practicing listening skills, note-taking skills, and speaking skills

Podcast
Resilience: Relationships are Key

Listen at
schoolofbelonging.org

Chapter 3
Empathy

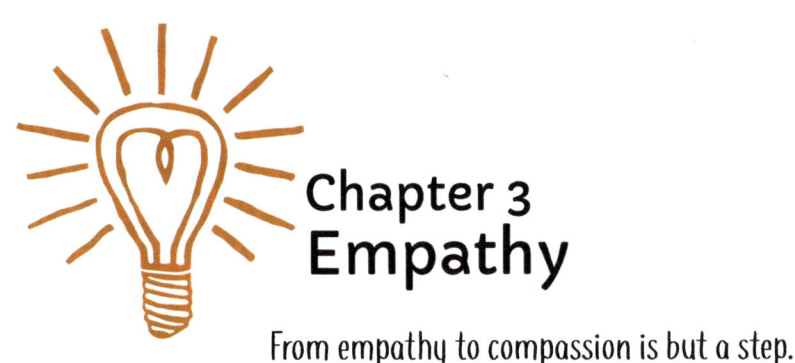

From empathy to compassion is but a step.

-Frederick Franck

Empathy Defined

In this chapter, I will present empathy as the ultimate pro-social skill that once activated sparks the intention of being present for our students as we absorb the humanity that exists within each of them. So often, when defining empathy, people describe it as "walking a mile in someone else's shoes," and while this is a worthy goal, I like to take the process further.

Adults never know when a moment with a student will be one the student never forgets—a positive emotional bookmark. Each day we have the opportunity to provide such positive moments for our students. Empathy as a practice is the touchstone by which teachers can guide the daily social decisions of students.

> adults never know when a moment with a student will be one the student never forgets— a positive emotional bookmark

Emotional Memories

Whenever a young person goes through an emotional event, whether it is positive or negative, chances are he or she will remember that event many years later. When one's emotions are touched, the heart has opened and change on a visceral level will occur. To emphasize the point that we remember emotional events, think about a time when you were very young (three to six years old) and you became separated from your parents somewhere in public (a store, a fair, a movie). Reflect for a moment on that event:

- How old were you?
- Where were you?
- Who were you with?
- What happened?
- How did you feel?
- Are there any other memories associated with that event?

Going through this exercise is an opportunity to internalize the notion that *emotion is learning*. Whenever we experience an emotional event, we will remember it.

This chapter focuses on creating emotionally coded social learning experiences that will imprint your students forever.

A Story and a Song

In 1986, as I was driving home from visiting my friend and colleague Marsha Brown through the back roads of Hampton, New Hampshire, I had an experience that would alter my life forever. I was listening to a tape of a song Marsha had just given me. The song told the true story of a boy named Howard Gray who was ridiculed and harassed by his peers because he was poor and not very articulate. Lee Domann, the songwriter, told the story from his point of view as the one who wanted to help this boy in some way but didn't have the courage to do so.

As I later discovered, Lee wrote Howard Gray on December 8, 1980, the night John Lennon was murdered outside of the Dakota Apartments in New York City. Lee wrote of his experience:

> *I, like many "children of the '60's," grieved the passing of an icon of our generation. . . . That night, as I thought back on those days, I found my mind moving further into the past. An unexpected memory suddenly emerged. It was that of a classmate from junior high school whom I had been guilty of laughing at as other students ridiculed and abused him. His name was Howard Ray. I had not seen or heard of him in twenty years. A deep remorse came over me. That night I wrote the music and [lyrics] to the song, "Howard Gray."*
>
> *At that time, I was living in Nashville, Tennessee, honing my craft as a commercial songwriter. The next morning, I looked over the lyrics and decided that no one would relate to the subject matter, so I threw it in the trash. A few hours later my wife, Maggie, was emptying the trash and found it. She said it was the best thing I had written and that I should keep it. She was right.*
>
> *The song began to get a very positive response at "writer's nights" along Music Row. It was the only one I had ever written that the audience grew dead silent every time I played it. I decided to change the name to "Howard Gray," as a gesture of trying to protect the real Howard's anonymity, though I thought the chances were very slim he'd ever hear it.*

leedomann.com/
howard_gray.html

The tape Marsha had given me was a collection of songs, which had been recorded by Gary Hall, a songwriter living in Nashville and performing at Music City at the same time as Lee Domann. One of those songs was *Howard Gray*.

Howard Gray

Most everyone I knew put the whole Gray family down

They were the poorest family in our little Kansas town

Howard always looked too big for his funny ragged clothes

The kids all laughed at him and Jimmy Jones would thumb his nose

Howard sat across from me in 7th grade at school

I didn't like it much but mama taught the golden rule

So when the spitballs flew at him I never would join in

I guess that was the reason Howard thought I was his friend

And after things would quiet down sometimes I'd turn and see

The grateful eyes of Howard Gray looking back at me

Howard Gray
Howard Gray

Somehow they got their kicks out of treatin' you that way

Deep down I kind of liked you but I was too afraid

To be a friend to you Howard Gray

One day after lunch I went to comb my hair and saw

They had Howard pinned against a locker in the hall

They were pokin' fun about the big hole in his shirt

They had his left arm twisted back behind him 'til it hurt

To this day I can't explain and I won't try to guess

Just how it was I wound up laughing harder than the rest

I laughed until I cried but through my tears I still could see

Teaching Empathy Institute

The tear stained eyes of Howard Gray looking back at me

Howard Gray
Howard Gray
I can't believe I joined them all in treatin' you that way
I wanted to apologize but I was too afraid
Of what they'd think about me Howard Gray

From that moment on after I made fun of him
He never looked my way
He never smiled at me again
And not much longer after that
His family moved away
And that's the last I ever saw or heard of Howard Gray
That was twenty years ago and I still haven't found
Just why we'll kick a brother or a sister when they're down
I know it may sound crazy but now and then I dream
About the eyes of Howard Gray lookin' back at me

Howard Gray
Howard Gray
I've never quite forgiven us for treatin' you that way
I only hope that somehow you'll hear this song someday
And you'll know that I am sorry Howard Gray

We'll probably never meet again
All I can do is pray
May you and God forgive us
Howard Gray

"Howard Gray"
©1992 Lee Domann
Shuretone Music
(BMI)

After listening intently to Hall's version of Howard Gray, I sensed how important that song could be in a school setting, and within two weeks I learned Howard Gray and sang it for my class of sixth-grade students. Once we got into the lesson, it was hard to stop. They wanted to keep talking about Howard. Why was he treated that way, and was the song really true? Over the next month, I was invited to share the song with other students in other classrooms in my school. The impact was immediate, and soon, there was a banner hanging in the foyer of our school, which read:

There will be no Howard Grays in this school!

Eventually, I found myself singing the song while conducting workshops in other schools and other states, in classes and workshop settings for students, teachers, and parents. Over time, I became known as "that guy who sings *Howard Gray*."

A Meeting

In hopes of making *Howard Gray* accessible to more people, I wanted to record the song. I contacted Lee Domann, who was delighted that I was sharing his song with students in schools. With his blessing, in 1987, I recorded *Howard Gray* and released it on a cassette in hopes that many more students (and teachers) would be touched and inspired to make a difference with others through Lee's moving expression.

In 1990, I wanted to take things further and decided to make a music video of the song, so I flew to Nashville to meet with Lee to discuss my idea of making a music video of *Howard Gray*. As he and I talked about the emotional power of his song, and of the potential impact a *Howard Gray* video could have, he suddenly shared that one month earlier, he had found Howard Ray in his home state of Kansas after almost thirty years. Even before Lee had finished telling me the story of their reconnection, I knew that we had to expand the video vision from a musical recreation of the song into a combination music video and documentary. He agreed.

Although I had never produced a music video, that night, as I lay awake, unable to contain my excitement, I wrote what I later learned was called a video treatment of the project in my journal. The vision of how the song would be expressed and staged (with student actors and then moving into the real visit) flowed out of me in a matter of minutes, and I knew we were creating something that would make a huge difference in the lives of the many young people in schools who were struggling to find their place of belonging.

Four months later, I flew to Lawrence, Kansas, with my videographer friend Tobe Carey. Lee drove to Kansas from Nashville and the three of us met at a local restaurant to set up for the shoot the next day. The plan was to have Lee and Howard meet outside the school where the story took place, go inside, walk through the halls, and settle into one of the classrooms. Once inside the classroom, they would sit across from each other in desks and reminisce about their school experiences.

As we shot the video the next day, it all went exactly as I had imagined. At one point the following exchange took place.

> **Lee:** All the time in my memory, I remember trying to be as much a friend to you as much as I could but not knowing how to do that. Did you know that? Did you know that I wanted to be a friend to you?
>
> **Howard:** No, I didn't.
>
> **Lee:** You were telling me earlier that you dropped out of school later on. Did it have to do with the way you felt?
>
> **Howard:** The way I was treated and everything, I didn't feel like going to school. I just wanted to stay at home.

Toward the end of the conversation, Lee recounted how he hadn't seen Howard in person for almost thirty years until the day Lee returned home to Kansas for his father's funeral. As Lee sat there in the church, he turned around to see Howard walking in to pay his respects. Howard's presence touched Lee greatly and inspired him to write a new ending to the song:

I thought we'd never meet again

   But at last now I can say

     You're a bigger man than I am, Howard Gray

I called the finished video *Through the Eyes of Howard Gray*.

Check out *Through the Eyes of Howard Gray* at schoolofbelonging.org

A Word

Prior to taping the *Howard Gray* video, in early December of 1989, while working as a visiting teacher for schools throughout the Northeastern United States, I had an unusual experience with a group of fifth-grade students. It was a snowy morning in Portland, Maine, and I was teaching a lesson called "Real-Life Conversations" at Longfellow Elementary School for the Portland City School District. I had just sung *Howard Gray* and I asked the students why others in school were often treated unfairly the way Howard was. As I turned to the blackboard, poised to record their answers, an image of a blank picture frame appeared in my mind. Inside the frame in bold, capitalized letters, I saw the word...

EMPATHY

I drew a frame on the board and wrote the word *EMPATHY* inside it exactly as I was seeing it in my mind. I stood there quietly for a moment and then said, "Please silently read the word I have written inside the frame." After a few

Teaching Empathy Institute

moments, I had a student read the word aloud for the class. I continued, "Empathy is being able to see inside someone else's 'picture,' understanding what he or she is going through and making caring choices based on what you see." Over the next thirty-five minutes a rich dialogue ensued in which we focused on compassion for others and the moral dilemmas people face every day over what is the caring choice when under social stress. When that lesson ended, I intuitively knew that empathy was to be the primary focus of my work as a teacher, workshop leader, and curriculum developer.

> although empathy seems to be about awareness for others, it's about having empathy for yourself, finding what brings you joy and meaning in your life as an educator

Since that fateful day in 1989, I have had numerous spirited conversations with colleagues on the topic of empathy. I have come away from these conversations with the perception that all people need to be conscious of how to manifest empathy in their own lives. It's a paradox, really, because although empathy seems to be about awareness for others, it's about having empathy for yourself, finding what brings you joy and meaning in your life as an educator, believing that you are here to express your uniqueness to the world through this role, and being open to what that expression might be.

It is an ancient concept that we need one another if we are to survive. Technology with all its magic, instant communication, and informational capability cannot provide the most basic emotional need: real-life human connection. Perhaps that is why there are an increasing number of people who feel cut off or removed from the human experience. Empathy is a journey of *remembering* the human heart. It is a core heart skill and cutting-edge practice for reconnection and self-discovery, and, teachers can facilitate it for students through focused, nonjudgmental listening when a student has a story to tell.

Shared Sorrow

Val Mihic, a former special education teacher, told me the following story that exemplifies what it takes to be an empathic teacher.

V. Mihic, personal communication, December 20, 2000

> *One year after returning from our holiday vacation, Michael, one of my students, was telling others in the class about the Nintendo game he had received for Christmas. It soon became apparent that Michael was not telling the others the truth; he really had not received a Nintendo. The other kids knew this as well and started to make fun of him. I sensed Michael's pain and I knew that he had a story to tell. I spoke with Michael privately asking him if he had in fact received a Nintendo for a gift. He said no and then told me how he hadn't received much for Christmas; his parents had an argument on Christmas Eve and his stepfather left the house that night. Michael said he didn't want the others to make fun of him so he made up the story of the Nintendo.*

Michael was too embarrassed and hurt to tell the truth about his meager and disappointing Christmas. He *made up* a story when in truth he needed the opportunity to *tell* his story. His teacher asked if he would like to talk to the class about the situation. Michael agreed. During a class meeting in which the class was seated in a focused circle, he told his true story. When Michael explained that his holiday had been a major disappointment for him, his classmates embraced him emotionally, saying such things to him as, "Don't worry about getting anything, Michael. You can use my Nintendo." Michael's teacher initiated this moment of group empathy with his empathic actions.

Empathy is an intuitive process that can be cultivated. It requires a person to be present when spending time with another and to listen. Being present in this context means coming into the relationship with the intention of caring—wanting to help the other person through listening, support, and encouragement. The fact that Val was present with his student is what caused him to

Teaching Empathy Institute

speak to Michael in the way he did. When a teacher is present for his or her students, this presence carries with it the opportunity for appreciation, thereby opening the door for an *empathic moment*—a moment that can be filled with the extremes of joy, elation, sorrow, and disappointment—shared between two individuals. The result of this empathic moment is summed up eloquently in the following Swedish proverb:

> *Shared joy is a double joy;*
> *Shared sorrow is half a sorrow.*

One empathic moment can significantly alter the course of a person's life, propelling him or her toward a new destination with a renewed sense of optimism and hope. When an incident has occurred with a student, there is always a story behind it—a sequence of events that led to the incident. When students are encouraged to share by their teacher, the teacher helps create a sacred or honorable climate in which teaching, learning, and community building occurs. It is the teacher's responsibility to intentionally create a setting in which storytelling—the sharing and *understanding* of other people's realities—is nurtured.

Listen to the song Mrs. Lopez I'll never forget you at schoolofbelonging.org

In the book *The Sacred: Ways of Knowledge, Sources of Life* (1977), Peggy V. Beck, A.L. Walters, and Nia Francisco write about the Lakota Sioux oral tradition of storytelling and how the Lakota consider storytelling to be the most significant practice for teaching the ways of the world and the ways of their people. I have found that learning about the traditions of the Native Americans has intrigued, opened up, and inspired many young people in my classes. Students find great fascination with the organic nature of happiness and purpose, which is embraced through the creation of and devotion to caring relationships toward one's self, others in the group or tribe, and the environment. In the Lakota tradition, most of the significant teaching and storytelling took place around the fire.

Beck, P.V., Walters, A.L., & Francisco, N. (1997). *The Sacred: Ways of knowledge, sources of life.* Tsaile, AZ: Navajo Community College Press.

The whole situation, the atmosphere around the fire, was dramatic—different from ordinary things like daily conversation and instruction. Maria Chona, a Papoga woman, explains how a child learned among her people: "My father went on talking to me in a low voice. This is how our people always talk to their children, so low and quiet, the child thinks he is dreaming. But he never forgets." (Beck, Walters, & Francisco, 1977, p. 60)

I am certain that Val's student Michael never forgot what his teacher did for him so many years ago. Val taught Michael that there is a place for each person and a place for each story. Michael's classmates learned this as well. Inviting Michael to share his story in a class meeting is analogous to the dramatic and different (and empathic) atmosphere Maria Chona described in her words about the Lakota tradition. Speaking in a low dreamlike voice symbolically means to intentionally create a nonjudgmental, emotionally safe teacher-student relationship that facilitates a learning environment where everyone feels an attachment to the group. It feels dreamlike because the feelings of safety, connection, and belonging are everyone's dream or desire.

The late Irish philosopher and poet John O'Donohue compared a person's life potential to a piece of clay that can be molded into any shape imaginable. Speaking figuratively, teachers who establish empathic relationships with their students will sense what types of "clay" each student represents and reflect this information back to the students, thereby helping each young person mold his or her unique shape, life expression, and future direction. Of life expression and self-trust, O'Donohue (2005) wrote:

johnodonohue.com

There is an unseen life that dreams us: it knows our true destiny. We can trust ourselves more than we realize and we need have no fear of change. We can risk everything for growth and we'll never be disappointed.

Teaching Empathy Institute

A Technique: The Listening Wheel

What it is
The listening wheel is a structured experience that is active, fun, and memorable.

How it is used
The listening wheel is used to teach and practice listening and to help students share their thoughts with many different classmates.

How to run one
Start out by having half of the class stand in a circle. Then have the other half go to the circle with each person standing behind another person from the inside circle. Those on the inside then turn around to face the people behind them, creating two circles: an inner circle and an outer one. The pairs of students are now ready to practice listening.

Review the three steps to listening:

1. Asking open-ended questions
2. Clarifying and summarizing
3. Reflecting feelings

Say that you will provide a question for each person on the inside circle to ask his or her partner on the outside circle. Once the person answers, those on the inside continue the dialogue by asking open-ended follow-up questions. They will continue until you stop them, which you will do using some type of signal (such as a hand motion, singing bowl, slide whistle, and so on).

Continued...

Once you stop them, instruct the listeners (the inside of the circle) to summarize back and share a reflection such as this:

> *I heard you say you love the morning because that is when you focus the best. It seems as if you love your alone time.*

After the summaries and reflections, reverse roles as the outside partners listen (ask questions) and the inside partners respond.

Once both partners have had a turn, rotate the outside circle two places so everyone has a new partner. Ask another question. Here is a sample sequence:

1. What is your favorite time of day?
2. What is something you do well?
3. What is a concern you have about school?
4. What do your friends like about you?
5. What would you like to be doing ten years from now?

The Listening Wheel is a technique, but it is also a process, meaning you can use it for any content. It is particularly useful and engaging to facilitate when reviewing information from your class, processing an experience, or practicing dialogue.

Specific purposes

- To practice listening
- To process classroom lessons or events
- To help students make connections with different students
- To have a novel experience

Partner Guidelines

After teaching listening to your students, introduce Partner Guidelines. One of the significant protective factors in social-skills development is learning how to work with partners effectively. Partner or pair work is a *protective factors learning experience*.

Process

Present partner guidelines in five steps posted on the wall:

1. Decide who goes first.
2. Ask three open-ended questions.
3. Share information you learned (summarize).
4. Reverse roles.
5. Report out to the class or in groups of four.

Once you present this process as a follow-up or application of listening, train your students to follow the posted guidelines. As this becomes routine, all you will say is the following:

Please get into partners. You have ten minutes (or whatever amount of time you provide).

Students will know what to do next.

Podcast:
The Artistry of Empathy: Creating the Conditions for Connection

Listen at schoolofbelonging.org

Field Guide to a School of Belonging

Chapter 4
Reflective Practice

> You can't connect the dots looking forward; you can only connect them looking backwards. So you have to trust that the dots will somehow connect in your future. You have to trust in something—your gut, destiny, life, karma, whatever.
>
> —Steve Jobs

Reflective Practice

One of the enlivening aspects of spending one's career in the field of education is the ever-present opportunity for personal and professional growth. The late Donald Schon, an organizational learning theorist and author, whose ideas influenced a generation of systems-change specialists, posited that a healthy learning organization is the outgrowth of reflective practice. He defined reflective practice as "the capacity to reflect on action so as to engage in a process of continuous learning" (Schon, 1983). The focus on continuous learning is key because it represents the challenge of doing things differently if current practices are not working as well as they could be. In the arena of social and emotional learning, reflective practice is evidenced through one of TEI's guiding practices, which states: *personal transformation creates systemic transformation.* A reflective practitioner steps back mindfully, seeking unique responses to everyday challenges, which over time leads to new ways of doing

Schon, D. A. (1983). The Reflective Practitioner: How professionals think in action. Cambridge, MA: Basic Books.

things. The field of education is one of the only professions where practitioners are not provided on a regular basis with opportunities to reflect on their practices and share with their colleagues what they have discovered. In the field of medicine, for example, if a doctor makes a discovery or feels frustration, he or she comes together with other doctors to explore what can be done and how things can be done better, collectively seeking to serve the greater good. This practice might serve to save a person's life.

Teachers who come together as a community of practice where group reflection and sharing of ideas is the norm might also be saving the life of a student, or at least helping to create a happier and more productive one. Whether in the classroom with students, a team room with committee members, or a faculty room with colleagues, reflective practice enhances the quality of the school experience, making it more positive, efficient, and effective. This chapter presents how reflective practice is infused into TEI's learning process.

> *a reflective practitioner steps back mindfully, seeking unique responses to everyday challenges, which over time leads to new ways of doing things*

Changing the Response

The first and probably most challenging step for the reflective practitioner to take is to look within at our tendencies and the internal struggles we have with students, colleagues, and parents. We will start by looking at the relationships a teacher has with students.

Answer this question:

What do kids do that drives you crazy?

The question is framed in this way because there are times when a student's behavior is confusing, frustrating, and emotionally draining. It is in these times when it is critical to analyze what responses are not working. In 1987, I heard educator and author Jack Canfield speak at an educational conference. In his talk, he presented the equation:

$$E + R = O$$

The event plus your response equals the outcome.

What Do Kids Do That Drives You Crazy?

jackcanfield.com

Since first hearing it, I have shared this little equation with many educators and parents with great impact in empathy workshops and training experiences. The critical practice is to focus your energies on the **R** of the equation. The only thing that will happen if you try to change the event or blame the event for what is happening is that you will feel frustration and eventually burnout. It is far more empowering and less stressful to articulate what you have control over in your life: the response.

As an educator, if you can determine what you do have influence over and focus your emotions there, you will not only be more effective but happier as well. In a *School of Belonging*, E + R = O is a symbol of the work we do every day. We can make a difference in the lives of our students. What derails us at times is when we take the behaviors of our students personally. Once this happens, our effectiveness wanes and our energy for the work is lessened.

Teaching Empathy Institute

Let's return to the question:

What do kids do that drives you crazy?

"Driving you crazy" is another way of saying that the actions produce an emotional reaction rather than a rational response. Emotional reactions to the behaviors that push your buttons can be traced back to some of the personal values that direct our lives.

Emotional Imprints

We learn personal values at a very young age from the people and events that surround us. These experiences are known as *emotional imprinting*, and they lay the architecture for the emotional structure of our lives. An imprint, like a tattoo, is a forever phenomenon. Imprints are non-negotiable and are most profound in the first fifteen years of life. They take the form of value statements or family mores and belief systems. Through the years, our imprints are embedded on our psyche; we are often unaware that they even exist.

An example of an imprint is punctuality. If it was instilled into you that you'd better be home for dinner on time or you would be in trouble, the imprinted value is that being on time is important and that punctuality is a sign of respect. A second imprint from this example is that it is important to eat dinner together as a family. Many years later, this trait of punctuality is perceived as a sign of integrity. People know they can count on you as someone who will always be on time. Additionally, if you have a family, you most likely hold the belief that it is important to have dinner together when you can. You place a high value on this. However, as with all things, there is the shadow side as well. The opposite experience plays out when a student arrives

> as an educator, if you can determine what you do have influence over and focus your emotions there, you will not only be more effective but happier as well

late to class or hands a paper in late. If your imprint is strong enough you might react from an emotional and irrational place and damage the relationship in the process. It is not about being right or wrong or letting go of the things important to you. It is about knowing not only what is important to you but also why you value this so much, and even deeper, what are the imprints of your students?

A quick litmus test for what your imprints are is to identify what your buttons or trigger points are. In other words, what do your students do that drives you crazy, and in the process, causes you to react in irrational or destructive ways? This same reflection can be applied to all of your professional relationships with colleagues, supervisors, and parents. If your imprints unconsciously drive you, you might not get the desired outcome from your professional relationships.

Again, the goal is not so much to change your imprints, but to make yourself aware of them. Even if upon reflection you reject certain imprints or belief systems from your childhood, in times of stress you often will return to what is most familiar, not necessarily what makes the most sense.

Emotional Intelligence

In 1990, researchers Peter Salovey and John D. Mayer published a highly influential article titled "Emotional Intelligence." In their work they define emotional intelligence (EQ) as, "The ability to perceive emotion, integrate emotion to facilitate thought, understand emotions, and to regulate emotions to promote personal growth" (Mayer & Salovey, 1997). Psychologist Daniel Goleman (1995) took the application of this work to another level with his book *Emotional Intelligence*, which

Salovey, P. & Mayer, J. D. (1990). Emotional intelligence. *Imagination, Cognition, and Personality*, 9, 185-211.

Mayer, J.D. & Salovey, P. (1997). What is emotional intelligence? In P. Salovey & D.J. Sluyter (Eds.), *Emotional Development and Emotional Intelligence: Educational implications* (p. 3-34). New York: Harper Collins.

created a national stir as to what EQ was and whether or not it could be taught.

In his book, Goleman articulated emotional intelligence as a "new kind of intelligence" that, if cultivated, could alter the emotional lives of people in profound and positive ways. He also theorized that children in contemporary culture had lower EQ because they had more opportunities for less social interaction. In *Emotional Intelligence,* Dr. Goleman highlighted specific school districts that were utilizing the research on emotional intelligence for a variety of programs and initiatives ranging from creating a caring classroom community to training students in conflict-resolution skills. His book made the point that schools need to place as much emphasis on emotional intelligence as they do on academic achievement, that in fact they are directly related.

Goleman, D. (1995). *Emotional Intelligence.* New York, NY: Bantam Books.

The entry point for developing one's EQ is self-awareness of how you respond toward others in stressful situations, in a way that enhances success and happiness in work and life. This takes a great deal of self-reflection. If you are going to feel safe in exploring new ways of responding, there needs to be the conditions of a supportive and nurturing school culture in which caring, compassion, and trust are the norm. When people feel connected within (understand how they feel and why) and then seek to create empathic and compassionate connections without, having healthy relationships with others, success and achievement will flourish because motivation will be high. EQ in practice helps people have what Dr. William Glasser (1990) calls a *needs-satisfying experience* (see Chapter 1), an experience in which a person's emotional needs are met.

Often, when people think of measuring a person's abilities and performance, IQ (intelligence quotient) is initially what comes to mind. IQ, which on some level is a part of the paradigm of standardization and high-stakes testing, lives at the surface in what is often considered to be the hard path toward gaining a competitive advantage. EQ lies beneath the surface, along what many consider to be the soft path. However, EQ skills are not soft at all but ultimately necessary, not only as a measurement of success, but also as an entry point to meaningful school, work, and life experiences.

Feedback

Feedback is a critical relationship- and community-building skill, and in its own way, models caring and belonging. Feedback is often confused with criticism or assertiveness, but it comes from a very different place and a different intention. The intention of feedback is to help an individual or group grow. It provides information that is observational: what was seen and what was heard and how those behaviors are affecting others, including yourself. It does not judge, label, minimize, or threaten. It is logical, specific, and useful.

There are two forms of feedback: negative or growth feedback and positive or status feedback.

Although positive feedback feels good, it is more helpful for personal and professional growth to receive negative or growth feedback. It may not feel good in the moment, but it is important to let a person or group know if what they are doing is counterproductive to a relationship or class experience.

Often, when an administrator, teacher, or other staff member gives negative feedback, it is expressed in the form of a "you" message as in, "You are being difficult." This is not feedback but judgmental and accusatory criticism, and it often takes place in front of others. Feedback feels and sounds very different. For example, "I feel frustrated when you interrupt. It seems as if you are dismissing my ideas. Please let me finish my thought before you share yours." Tone and volume of voice combined with physical proximity to another is just as critical when giving feedback. If you speak in quiet and relaxed tones, with strong eye contact, while giving the recipient some space and boundaries, and you deliver the message with a compassionate intention, you will most likely be giving productive and helpful feedback. If, on the other hand, your emotions get the better of you, you take the behavior personally, and you become angry and

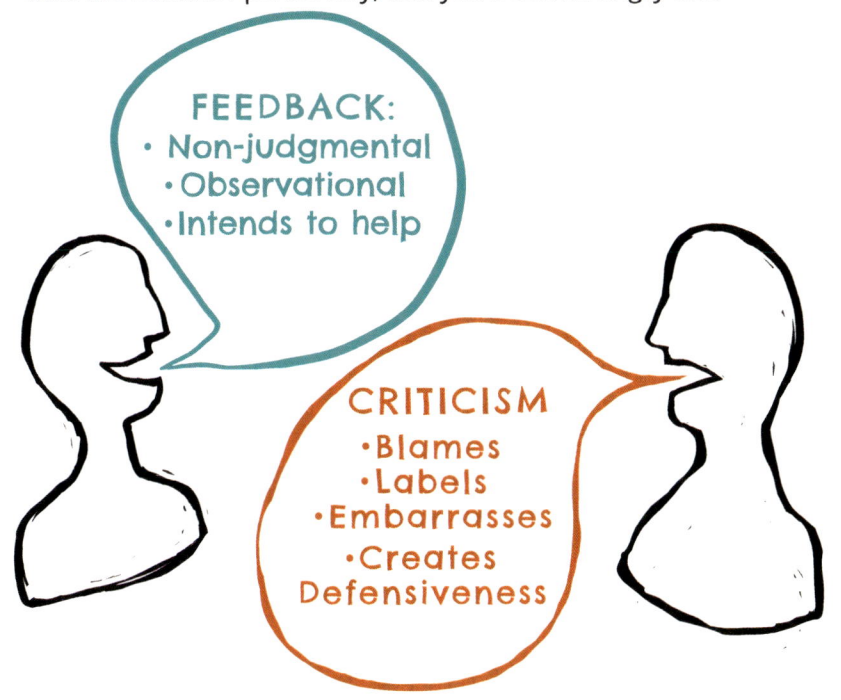

FEEDBACK:
- Non-judgmental
- Observational
- Intends to help

CRITICISM
- Blames
- Labels
- Embarrasses
- Creates Defensiveness

upset as you are trying to stop a behavior, or even become sarcastic in doing so, the student will most likely shut down, become defiant, or escalate in his emotions and behaviors.

A simpler way to look at feedback is that it is a form of high-level listening. If you have a feedback mindset, when a person is telling you something, you will invite thoughts in non-judgmentally, ask questions to learn more, and summarize back for clarity and understanding. The summary is not an exact replay but rather a reflection of what jumps out to you as the listener. This form of feedback is the essence of what I explore in the next section: dialogue.

Field Guide to a School of Belonging

Dialogue: The art of collective thinking

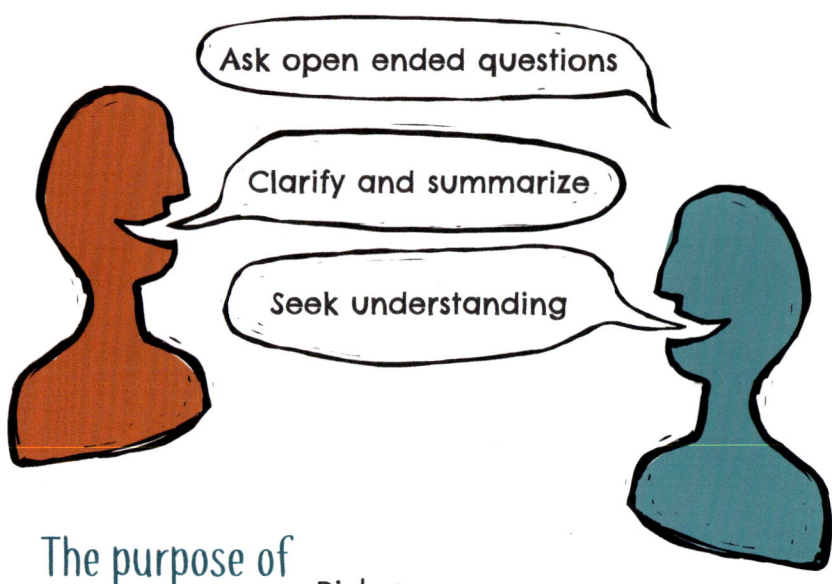

- Ask open ended questions
- Clarify and summarize
- Seek understanding

> The purpose of dialogue is not necessarily to come to an agreement, but rather to come to an understanding of all points of view

Bohm, D. (1996). *On Dialogue.* New York, NY: Routledge.

Dialogue

Physicist and scholar David Bohm is the person from whom I first learned about dialogue as a group reflective tool. Much like Donald Schon's (1983) vision that people can demonstrate learning by altering old habits or responses, dialogue helps people challenge their assumptions as they interact and listen to others. The purpose of dialogue is not necessarily to come to an agreement, but rather to come to an understanding of all points of view, thereby creating a common thread of connection within the group through collective thinking. This is achieved through high-level listening. In high-level listening, as a team member (or student) speaks, all others focus on what he or she is saying, following up with open-ended questions. These questions begin with who, what, where, when, and how, and invite more information. These questions are interspersed with summary statements to clarify for understanding.

Teaching Empathy Institute

A group or team that practices dialogue has high *group emotional intelligence*. Many team meetings can rapidly become stressful, and at its best, dialogue tends to mitigate the interpersonal issues or conflicts that may surface. It is a natural step for the group or class to flow from dialogue toward what is referred to as *skillful discussion*, where group members make hard decisions, take positions, and create a plan. Dialogue as an instructional practice, team process, or assessment tool is one of the cornerstone practices within a *School of Belonging*.

Resonance

As educators intentionally build connecting, trusting, and safe relationships with their students, in the process they are creating positive, meaningful, and everlasting emotional memories for those students. If the process of intentional emotional imprinting grew to become a cultural norm practiced by all in a *School of Belonging*, then all students and staff would feel good about being in school on most days. This positive emotional meter is the demonstration of what some of the literature on group dynamics would call *group resonance*.

In the book Primal Leadership: Learning to Lead with Emotional Intelligence, Daniel Goleman and his colleagues (2002) define resonance as "a reservoir of positivity that brings out the best in people" (p. ix). Resonance is not a program or process; it starts with an intention that focuses on the positive energy that flows and the high achievement attained when people in a learning organization honor and trust one another. It's like the feeling a person gets when he or she is experiencing something he or she loves. This could be a visit to a family vacation spot, a hike to a special place in the woods, the look on the face of your child when she is happy, a room in your home where you can find some peace and solace, or a favorite song or performer.

Goleman, D., Boyatzis, R., & McKee, A. (2002). *Primal Leadership: Learning to lead with emotional intelligence.* Boston, MA: Harvard Business School Press.

If a school is a place where resonant moments are the norm, amazing and magical things will happen. Renee Levi (2006, p. 2), who has studied resonance in organizations, notes:

> *Occurrences of resonance between individuals and within groups happen every day in situations in which people come together and experience intimacy and bonding, a felt sense of being in the flow or transcending, personal transformation, and sometimes the satisfaction of accomplishing extraordinary things. (p.2)*

If, through the deep connection a resonant experience provides, a school can encourage students toward their growing edge where academic learning, social and emotional development, and unique expression is attained, then a resonant *School of Belonging* must be the primary intention for where we want our students to be every day.

Levi, R. (2006). Group Magic: An inquiry into experiences of collective resonance. Reflections: *The SOL Journal*, 6 (Feb/March), p.2.

A Technique: The Check-In

What it is
The check-in a simple form of dialogue that facilitates immediate connection between two or more people who will be working together.

How it is used
The check-in is used whenever a meeting begins, or a class starts. It allows everyone to focus and be present, leaving all stresses at the door.

How to run one
At the beginning of a meeting or class, provide everyone in the group with an opportunity to state how he or she is doing, as in, "What's going on for you right now?" or "How are you doing with this new curriculum we are implementing?"

After each person shares, the facilitator or leader of the group summarizes back some of the key points that were shared.

This might seem like a simple technique, but it can be extremely meaningful and connecting. Often, when someone shares something he or she is upset about, or shares that he or she is just not feeling well, that person will feel better for having freed himself or herself of something that was brewing inside. Other times, someone can call for a check-in in the middle of a meeting or class to determine how everyone is doing.

The check-in only takes five to ten minutes, and it is time well spent.

Specific Purposes
- To see how everyone is doing
- To set the tone for the class or meeting
- To model how to value the relationship before the task
- To practice group reflection

Appreciative Inquiry

Appreciative inquiry is a type of focus group that highlights celebration, appreciation, and support. Often when staff members take part in an open focus group, the energy quickly spirals downward, ending up in venting, complaining, and negativity. The purpose of a focus group, which is to provide an understanding of current realities, gets lost in the pessimistic landscape, and people end up feeling bad about their school or organization. A more desired effect comes about by framing the group as a celebration of pride and appreciation for being a staff member in the school. Appreciative inquiry pursues possibilities by focusing on the core strengths that exist within a school and its staff. This is an asset approach (as opposed to a deficit approach) and lends itself to positive forward movement where creative planning and problem-solving emerge.

Here are some appreciative inquiry openings:

- Talk about a time when you felt proud about being a staff member of this school.
- Share a recent success you had with a student.
- How can we celebrate all that we do here?
- Share one positive piece of feedback for a person in our group.
- What next steps can we take?

Appreciative inquiry by its very nature also facilitates organic team-building because it builds bonds of support, acceptance, and appreciation.

Podcast:
Emotional Imprinting: A Road map to Understanding Ourselves and Others

Teaching Empathy Institute

Afterword

A central theme of a *School of Belonging* is that it is a place where one's emotional needs are met, where story-telling and conversation are a part of the process, and where all stories are celebrated. When a school is emotionally safe, and when the staff and students receive training and workshop experiences relevant to their own social and emotional learning needs, resonance will be a cultural norm and will generate the inspiration, creativity, and discovery necessary for forward thinking that is positive and caring. My hope is that what I have written and recorded (podcasts and songs) for this field guide will resonate with you, inspiring you to make a difference with your colleagues and in the lives of the students with whom you work every day.

I encourage you to act on what you have learned from reading and working with the field guide. One of the greatest gifts an educator possesses is the opportunity to touch a child's world each day in ways that will affect that person for the rest of his or her life. We never know when a moment in time with a student will be a moment forever. I wish you all the best as you continue to be a significant adult in the lives of your students.

David Levine
Stone Ridge, NY
September, 2018

**Closure Podcast:
Simplicity: Simple Does Not Mean Trivial**

Listen at
schoolofbelonging.org

David Levine is an educator, writer, and musician with more than thirty-five years of experience working in a multitude of educational settings as a teacher, community builder, and social and emotional learning specialist. David has worked with school districts throughout the United States and beyond, focusing on creating caring and compassionate school cultures where social and emotional learning and emotional intelligence are foundational belonging and relationship-building practices.

As a musician, songwriter, producer, and podcast host, David uses his songs and digital materials as learning tools, including the Music Dialogue Process, which inspires both children and adults to look within to make a positive difference with others. As a writer, he has authored six books and numerous journal articles and curricula materials that focus on empathy and emotional intelligence practices as community building and leadership tools. He is currently producing a documentary film on his empathy work with children and adults in schools and communities throughout the world.

photo: Jodi Palinkas

Teaching Empathy Institute creates tailor-made programs designed to foster dialogue about social culture building while strengthening the capacity for the infusion of empathy and compassion into all aspects of the learning experience. If you would like to learn more about our professional development initiatives and digital learning tools, please check out our website:

www.teachingempathyinsitute.org

References

Bandura, A. (1997). *Self-Efficacy: The Exercise of Control.* New York, NY: W. H. Freeman and Company.

Beck, P.V., Walters, A. L., & Francisco, N. (1977). *The Sacred: Ways of knowledge, sources of life.* Tsaile, AZ: Navajo Community College Press.

Bogenschnieder, K., Small, S., & Reily, D. (1991). *National Extension Youth at Risk: An ecological, risk-focused approach for addressing youth at-risk issues.* Chevy Chase, MD: National 4-H Center, Wisconsin Extension.

Bohm, D. (1996). *On Dialogue.* New York: Routledge.

Cooper, R. K., & Sawaf, A. (1997). *Executive EQ: Emotional Intelligence in Leadership and Organizations.* New York: Berkley.

Domann, L. (1992) *Howard Gray* (song), Shuretone Music (BMI).

Glasser, W. (1990). *The Quality School: Managing Students Without Coercion.* New York, NY: Harper Perennial.

Goldstein, A. P., (1999). *The Prepare Curriculum: Teaching Pro-social Competencies.* Champaign, IL., Research Press.

Goleman, D. (1995). *Emotional Intelligence.* New York, NY: Bantam Books.

Goleman, D. , Boyatzis, R., & McKee, A. (2002). *Primal Leadership: Learning to Lead with Emotional Intelligence.* Boston, MA: Harvard Business School Press.

Goleman, D., & Senge, P. (2014). *The triple focus: A new approach to education.* Florence, MA: More Than Sound.

Kessler, R. (2000). *The soul of education: Helping students find connection, compassion, and character at school.* Alexandria, VA: ASCD.

Levi, R. (2006). Group Magic: An Inquiry into Experiences of Collective Resonance. *Reflections: The SOL Journal*, 6(2/3).

Levine, D. A. (2018). *Can you hear me? Listening to the voices of children,* CD. Stone Ridge, NY. Teaching Empathy Press.

Levine, D. A. (2006). *The school of belonging plan-book.* Bloomington, IN: Solution Tree Press.

Levine, D. A. (2005). *Teaching Empathy: A blueprint for caring, compassion, and community.* Bloomington, IN: Solution Tree Press.

Levine, D.A. (2003). *Building classroom communities: Strategies for developing a culture of caring.* Bloomington, IN: Solution Tree Press.

Levine, D.A. (1998). *Through the Eyes of Howard Gray* Video. Accord, NY: Blue Heron Press.

Levine, D. A., Kreitzer, J. (1995). *The Peer Partners Handbook: Helping your friends live free from violence, drug abuse, teen pregnancy, and suicide.* Barrytown, NY: Station Hill Press.

Mayer, J.D. & Salovey, P. (1997). What is emotional intelligence? In P. Salovey & D.J. Sluyter (Eds.), *Emotional Development and Emotional Intelligence: Educational implications.* New York: Harper Collins.

Minahan, J. & Rappaport, N. (2013). *The Behavior Code: A practical guide to understanding and teaching the most challenging students*. Boston, MA: Harvard Education Press.

Olweus, D. (1993). *Bullying at school: What we know and what we can do.* London: Wiley-Blackwell Publishing.

Salovey, P. , Mayer, J. D. (1990). Emotional intelligence. *Imagination, Cognition, and Personality*, Sage Journals 9.

Schon, D. A. (1983). *The Reflective Practitioner: How Professionals Think in Action*. Cambridge, MA: Basic Books.

Senge, P., Kleiner, A., Roberts, C., Ross, R., & Smith, B. (1994). *The Fifth Discipline Fieldbook*. New York, NY: Currency, Doubleday.

Wenger, E., McDermott, R., Snyder, W. (2002). *Cultivating Communities of Practice*. Boston, MA: Harvard Business School Press.

Werner, E. E., & Smith, R. S. (1992). *Overcoming the Odds: High Risk Children from Birth to Adulthood.* Ithaca, NY: Cornell University Press.

Williamson, M. (2002). *Everyday grace: Having hope, finding forgiveness, and making miracles*. New York, NY: Riverhead Books.

Appendix

Podcast Transcripts

Chapter 1 Podcast
Emotional Safety: A Blue Print For Success

Today we're going to focus on emotional safety. We all know what physical safety is. Emotional safety is a little more challenging to understand, but it's critical as we work with our children in school. We all have needs–we have physical needs (food, shelter), but we also have emotional needs. Now physical needs are much easier to meet for a child. If a child is hungry, we feed them. And the reason we do that is because, if someone's hungry, they can't focus on anything else. If someone is cold, they can't focus on anything else except "Why is it so cold, I need a jacket, I have to warm up." Those are physical needs and we can change things around–feed the children in school, get them jackets to wear outside at recess. Those are physical needs, and we can meet them. The emotional needs are very different, and by understanding what they are, we can learn what I would call the blueprint for emotional safety.

Now according to psychologist William Glasser, he says that there are four emotional needs. The first emotional need is the need to belong, to have a place, to be affiliated. The second emotional need is power and this means competence, this means "I'm good at something." When someone is really good at something, usually they really enjoy doing it, so their motivation is going to be very, very high. That's an emotional need–to feel like I have a purpose in life. To feel that I can help others would be an example of power. The third emotional need is freedom, and in context of the classroom, a freedom means to have voice. Freedom means that the adult in the classroom, the teacher or other adults in the school, really want to know what that child thinks, what that child feels, what ideas they might have. And by inviting those ideas in, you're providing the emotional need for

Field Guide to a School of Belonging

freedom. The fourth emotional need is fun. And by fun I mean to be engaged, to be engaged in the learning experience.

I recently attended a science fair of my son at his high school, and all the students had been working in teams and they had done a research project. And they made a presentation and we walked around and heard these presentations. The thing that struck me was how engaged they were. They were excited, they were lit up, and it was obvious that they were teaching what they had learned. And that was fun for them. It met their emotional need. Again, the four emotional needs are: belonging, power, freedom, and fun. When these are met, the motivation of the child will be very, very high. When these are met, we have created the blueprint for emotional safety.

William Glasser says that when the emotional needs are met, this is called the "quality world" or the "quality school." And he defines the quality world for all of us, as that place where every memory we've ever had that was joyful, where those memories reside – it could be a favorite vacation spot, it could be a favorite song or a relationship with an adult that we had while growing up – if that relationship, if that place, if that song, met those needs of belonging, power, freedom, and fun, those joys become the quality world. And we as adults can facilitate emotional safety by being quality world people in the lives of our students.

Musical Interlude....

The word facilitate is a very common phrase, but I'd like to explain what it means in this context. To facilitate means to make easy and if we focus on meeting the emotional needs of our students, we can make the meeting of those needs easy by going into something called high level listening.

Listening is such a simple term, but simple does not mean trivial. Simple actually means very deep and focused. And there are three things we can do as adults to be high-level listeners as we meet the emotional needs of our students. The first thing we can do is to ask them questions: who, what, where, when, how? Facilitate an exploration. Facilitate an understanding. Meet their need for freedom, for voice, by inviting them to tell their story. Every child has a story and if we can ask them the questions to facilitate the telling of that story, we also are facilitating belonging, power, freedom, and fun. Be very conscious not to ask a "why" question because "why" often, unintentionally, puts children into a defensive place. So ask open-ended questions to draw out information as the first step to high-level listening.

Once we get information, we can then reflect it back – that's called summarizing, but take it up a notch – clarify and summarize. Clarify means to make sure I understood what you said. "Here's what I heard." You repeat it back. It's showing the child that you're present and that you care for them. That's what a quality world adult would do. The highest level response to give to a child, to facilitate emotionally safe relationships, and to facilitate an emotionally safe learning environment, is to reflect back what they feel. Not to tell them what they feel, not even to interpret, but to reflect back what you're sensing. If you're truly present, you will figure this out. And if you're not correct, they'll correct you. So "wow, that must have been really upsetting to you" or "wow, that must have been so exciting when that happened." And then that will engage them. Right? Fun. And then they'll continue to tell their story and you can continue to ask questions. Now this sounds so easy. It is not. This is a critical relationship building skill: asking open ended questions, clarifying and summarizing, and reflecting feelings. By doing this, not only are we building a relationship, but we are teaching this as a critical pro-social skill to our students by modeling it and, in the process, building an emotionally safe learning community.

Chapter 2 Podcast
Resilience: Relationships Are Key

Today we're going to talk about the issue of resilience. Now I know so many people have heard about this term, but I'd like to give it to you in a very operational way.

First, let's start with the definition for children. A resilient child has hope and optimism for the future. They're flexible and they can maneuver through life's challenges in a way where they can learn and grow from them and help others in the process. The framework that I learned about resilience from, was from two researchers from the University of California: Ruth Smith and Emmy Werner. And the two of them conducted a study that they called "Children of the Garden Isle." They focused on young people on the island of Kuai in the Hawaiian Islands, and they targeted children who were born into very difficult situations in their lives, in their homes and in their communities. And as these children grew into school age, they looked at what was happening once they entered the school experience and they found that some of these children through the years who had very challenging emotional life situations, some of these children grew in to very happy productive successful adults, while others did not. And they wanted to articulate what was the difference in their experience - in their experience with adults in their lives in school, adults in their lives in their communities. What changed for them? What impacted their life trajectory? And what they came to were two types of what they called "protective factors": external and internal.

The external protective factors are the factors that we as the adults in the lives of our students can have direct influence over. Really they're the conditions that we intentionally create in our schools and in our communities. They're the relationships that we cultivate with our children, basically creating an emotionally safe learning environment. Once those are in place we can look to the internal protective factors. Now Emmy Werner called pro-social skills the "great protectors." And that's critical here in our work because a child who has pro-social skills has the ability to make connections that are healthy with their peers, can maneuver through the various challenges that all of our relationships pose.

Children who do not have pro-social skills, children who are not able to communicate what their thinking and what they're feeling, often demonstrate their communication through their behaviors–often antisocial behaviors. So our challenge as adults is to facilitate learning opportunities for our students where we first decode their behaviors to understand what they need. And then through our relationship, help move them to another place in their life that is healthy and happy, and in the process teach them the pro-social skills that they will need.

Teaching Empathy Institute

Appendix

So, there are two mechanisms we're going to look at to do so – two mechanisms to look at how to build resilience for our students. The first is kind of a general overarching vision and that is called the micro-interaction. Micro-interactions are the most effective and efficient ways to build resilience for our children. Another way of saying this is "the little things are the big things." Little moments in a child's life can absolutely become memories they never forget for the rest of their life. It could be a comment we make at just the right time, something we notice, something we acknowledge that will stay with them. It becomes an emotional memory. Emotion is learning.

I remember one year when I was teaching sixth grade. It was the first day of school and one of my students came in the very first day, the very beginning of the school day – her name is Heather – and I looked at Heather and she said "good morning" and I looked, and I noticed that over the summer she'd gotten her braces. And I said "Heather you have braces, those look really cool" and she said "Thank you, Mr. Levine". It was a little interaction, it came and it went – it was a micro-interaction. The next day her mother came into my classroom before the day and said how Heather could not stop talking about how excited she was that her teacher noticed her braces. This was a life event for her that was really huge and she was uncertain coming in, and I just kind of noticed it and made a comment. That is an example of a micro-interaction.

Another very specific strategy of the micro-interaction is called the two-by-ten strategy. Many children, those who don't have the pro-social skills, those often who don't have the ability to say what they need or what they're feeling, their behavior is they will disconnect from the group, they will disconnect from their peers. Or it might be a child who doesn't have a lot of friends. Or it might be a child who you, yourself as the adult, have a hard time making connections with. Think of one of those children, a child you know, hopefully within your class, but it could be someone in your school, and for ten days in a row give that child two minutes of uninterrupted, positive, focused attention. Engage them in conversation – not about school, not about their grades or their study habits, but about them as a person. Focus on them. Give them that unconditional positive connection, that unconditional positive regard that builds an emotionally safe relationship with you the teacher. That is called the two-by-ten strategy.

If you do this, after ten days, you will notice a shift in the affect of that child, a shift in the way they carry themselves throughout the school day, particularly when you're interacting with them. If you think about adults from your own life, adults who you have positive emotional memories about – school teachers, coaches, counselors, people from your community – if you think about someone who is positive, who had a positive impact on you, reflect on two things: how did you feel when you were in their presence? And how would you describe that person? Those were protective factors people – those were people who helped create resilience along the way. We're all resilient, we've all had challenging situations in our lives and yet every one of us woke up this morning and moved into our day. We're resilient – we've sprung back from the various challenges we've had. And a great gift for a child is to be that significant adult who can create resilient experiences.

Chapter 3 Podcast
Artistry of Empathy

Today we're going to talk about the Artistry of Empathy. And I see empathy as really an art form because it's about building relationships, and relationship building, and building healthy relationships, really is an art form. And empathy is the portal into building healthy, caring, and compassionate connections with others.

So we're going to explore how I've taken this idea of empathy – empathy as an art form, as an imaginative process – and brought that into my learning sessions with students in the hopes that you'll be able to see how you can utilize it in your work with your children as well.

From the very beginning when I started to speak with educators about empathy, the conversation was always around, first is it something you can teach, secondly are there skills involved? So often people stop when they use the very common descriptor for empathy "walking a mile in someone else's shoes", "feeling what they're feeling". And I think that's an awesome beginning to the process, but I

Appendix

like to take it much further into asking people to step back, feel what someone else is feeling (having that intention), but then also to have the skills and the reflection abilities to do something about those feelings that you're taking in. So, this is something as teachers we can teach very concretely, through our own modeling, through our own behaviors and responses to children – particularly those who are in distress.

Musical Interlude....

I want to tell you a story that's the story of a friend of mine. His name is Bob. And Bob was a person I met my first year teaching and I had his son Gregory in my fourth grade class. And Bob told me the story of when he was in third grade, his family lived in the city of Niagara Falls. And at the end of that school year, probably in May, they moved to another community within the city. So, they were still in Niagara Falls, but it was a whole new group of children and it was a new school with new teachers. A lot of stress going on for him. And he said that he didn't particularly like his new school, and he didn't think the teacher liked him and he didn't like her. So, it was kind of a negative experience. When he entered fourth grade, he had this teacher named Mrs. Arens and Bob still felt disconnected from the school experience from his previous year, and so he was the class clown in his words. He acted out and didn't always do what he was told to do by his teacher. Well one day Mrs. Arens walked up to Bob and she said "you know Bob I've noticed you're a great reader and you're also really interested in history" and Bob was thinking "I didn't know that about myself. How does she know that I'm a good reader? And I'm good in history? Huh." And then she continued and said "You know Bob, I have this book it's called Kit Carson Frontiersmen – I think you might be interested in it." So she gave him the book and he brought it home. The next morning when Bob came into school, Mrs. Arens walked up to him and she asked him "Did you have a chance to look at that book?" and he said "Not only did I look at it, I read the whole thing." And she had Bob then share with the class what he had learned, celebrating him, integrating him into the school experience.

She then said "You know Bob I've noticed that you have really nice handwriting. You know we're going to have this handwriting contest, I think you should enter." So, Bob spent two weeks practicing his penmanship and then put his entry in. Not only did he win the classroom contest, he won the school wide handwriting contest and his paper was in a window glass case in the front of the school when you entered. That really shifted his life experience. He became really interested in history and reading, and was meticulous with his handwriting. Many many years later he became a teacher, a social studies teacher, and his first teaching job was in that same Niagara Falls School District. And in the beginning of the year they had a Superintendent's Conference Day and Mrs. Arens still taught in the district. He walked up to her and said, "My name is Bob Barrett and I was a student in your fourth grade class, and I won the penmanship contest that year." and she said "Sit down young man, I have something I want to tell you." She said, "That was the first and only penmanship contest we ever had in the school." And really what she did was she saw this child who had some unmet needs, and she created the conditions for him to find some success, some celebration. He was probably the only entrant in that handwriting contest, but what she did was to practice empathy. She absorbed his experience. She listened to him, and created an experience that would provide him with success. And that is the Artistry of Empathy – building that relationship, helping a child to un-earth their unique gift and talent to the world, by holding a mirror up, reflecting back to them what is amazing about them. And in the process, teaching them to be empathic themselves.

In fact, it was Bob who took me under his wing when I was a new teacher and helped me see the value that I could provide for students and for teachers. So, Mrs. Arens lived through Bob, to me, and hopefully the children who you work with will have a similar experience. That's what empathy is. It's not just feeling what someone else is feeling. It's tuning into them, absorbing it, and making some conscious choices of what steps that you can take to help create a greater sense of connection to themselves and to each other. It's kind of like a humanistic version of differentiation. We talk about differentiated learning – well, as an adult with children, we can differentiate our responses to them, finding the unique pathway to meet their needs. That is empathy in practice. And as I said, it's also a way of teaching it. It's a harnessing of the natural inclination we have to be caring, kind, and compassionate people, and surround that inclination with a series of skills and strategies. We can teach our students to do the same thing. And that is the Artistry of Empathy.

Appendix

Chapter 4 Podcast
Emotional Imprinting: A Roadmap to Understanding Ourselves and Others

Today we're going to look at something called emotional imprinting and the impact that our imprints have on the relationships that we establish in our lives whether it's with our students or adults who we are with every day.

From the moment we're born, right up until we're fifteen years old or so, we have very strong imprinting experiences from the other people in our lives. These imprints create our value system or the things that are important to us, the things we value. An example might be punctuality – if your father was really, really intense about "you have to be on time, you have to be on time, we can't be late" that was driven into you as something that was important, something to value. So now it becomes part of my value system that punctuality means that you're being respectful, it's really important. Now if I'm a teacher and a student comes in late to my class, I now have a challenge: do I respond rationally or react emotionally? Our imprints will get in the way of responding rationally.

Another example of an imprint might be around respect. Maybe you were taught when you were growing up that children need to respect adults and that's really important to me and I teach my own children this. I value it. But what if I'm teaching and a student says "you know you got that answer wrong Mr. Levine, you wrote the wrong answer." Rather than responding rationally and saying "Wait let's look at that maybe, I did," I might react emotionally and say "that's not being respectful" and suddenly there's a disconnect. There is no relationship of safety and trust. Instead there is an environment of fear that is created by that.

So the point is that we all have imprints, every one of us. We didn't choose them, they were the ones we experienced and they're non-negotiable. And many times they're invisible to us. So, what's critical is to step back and reflect and ask ourselves what is important to me? What are my imprints? Now one really quick way of doing so is to make a list of all of the things that happen that trigger your angry behaviors. Sometimes we call these buttons – things, when they're pushed, we react emotionally. I already said punctuality is an example of one, respect for adults is one. Another example would be language – you know the language that a child uses – profanity for instance.

And the point is that what my imprints are, are not necessarily the ones that our children have. So we might be in a situation in our class and a child is sitting there and says something or acts in a certain way that pushes our button. And if we're not careful we enter into something called the conflict cycle and it kind of goes like this: the child is sitting there, maybe they're unsure of what's going on, maybe they feel dumb or they don't feel that you've been teaching it properly, so they might feel stress. That stress creates a feeling: "I resent this teacher; I don't like this subject; I hate this class; I don't have any friends here." Those are feelings. Those feelings drive behaviors. They might cut up, they might make jokes, they might call out, they might laugh. At that moment, your response to that behavior is what's most critical. And if you're not aware of your imprints, if you're not managing your imprints, you get into an interface issue. They have one set of imprints which might be about survival in a stressful learning situation and you have an imprint that says they need to be respectful – "I'm the teacher and they need to listen to me." If we react to that imprint and raise our voice and label their behavior "you're being rude, you're being disrespectful," we've now entered into something called the conflict cycle because our reaction creates another stressful event, which creates another feeling, which creates another behavior, and there's no way to get out of that conflict cycle. The child will win every single time.

So, if we are able to step back, not when it's happening, but when we have time to reflect. You know there's the old joke about the guy standing on his field and it's raining outside and his neighbor comes over and complains because his roof is leaking. He says "My roof is leaking, I don't know what to do – it's getting all wet in my house right now. I have to fix that thing." And the next day it's sunny out and you see your neighbor and you say "Aren't you going to fix your roof?" He says "No, I don't have to, it's not raining." The point is, you fix the roof when it's sunny. The point is, you reflect on your imprints when you're not in the situation. You build the relationship with the child when it's not stressful. You create new imprints about the relationship that that child has with you – the imprint of trust; the imprint that this adult cares about me, listens to me; that this adult, this teacher, likes me. We can intentionally build imprints for our students within our classrooms, within our relationships. And we can do so more effectively if we one, identify our own emotional imprints and two, come up with strategies to manage them when they occur.

You know, Stephen Covey, one of the things he speaks of in his book The Seven Habits of Highly Effective People is something he calls "emotional bank accounting." And his point is that we have to invest in relationships. We have to build that sense of trust, build that sense of belonging and connection. And so when there is a stressful event and we have to make a withdraw from the relationship, we want to make sure we have more on the plus side, so that we don't destroy the relationship, but actually build on it. That's fixing the roof when it's sunny. That's building new imprints with our students, for our students, and managing our own imprints along the way.

Afterword Podcast
Simplicity: Simple Does Not Mean Trivial

Today we're going to talk about simplicity. Now I know in previous podcasts I've explored the quote "simple does not mean trivial," but I was inspired to revisit this idea while thinking about a conversation I had a couple of years ago with a friend and colleague named Claudia Madrazo. Claudia is from Mexico and she's an educator, an artist, a conservationist, an author. Claudia is many amazing things, but the simple focus of her work is that we can create the conditions for children where they can find their unique voice that resides inside, and provide opportunities for them to express it to the world and make a difference. It's a creative process. And much like Claudia's form of art that's a creative process, I see social and emotional learning as a similar creative process. For it's a consciousness. Everything starts from a way of thinking–that focused, simple way of seeing the world. And Claudia, on her website, writes about consciousness in a very, very beautiful and elegant way. This is what she says. "Active consciousness is the capacity to observe, direct, and transform thoughts, emotions, and behaviors in order to manifest new possibilities."

New possibilities. This work we do with the children in our schools, with the children in our classrooms, provides the palette for new possibilities, for more opportunities for self-expression and for safer learning environments. That's the essence of what we mean by simple does not mean trivial and today we'll explore how simplicity is a pathway to transformation. And we'll refocus on some of the simple ideas that I've previously shared – things like ritual, common language, predictability, consistency, and group norms setting.

Musical Interlude....

I recently had a planning meeting with the superintendent of a large school district. And we came to the realization that, with all of the conversation in schools around such things as graduation rates, test scores, and teacher evaluation, social and emotional learning often is left standing in the shadows of the conversation. We agreed that SEL needs to be activated as a practice by talking about it as part of the daily conversation. It needs to be taken out of the shadow and moved into the light so that people know what SEL is, so people know how to synthesize it into a living and breathing way of doing what we do every day in our schools, every day in our communities, as we guide mentor and inspire children.

So let's break things down to their simplest form and map out how to synthesize these ideas. The simple vision that I hold is for students to be happy, honorable, and respectful.

In order for this to manifest, we need to understand that needs drive behaviors. And the emotional needs of belonging, power, freedom, and fun are where we need to start as we hold the intention of creating emotionally safe learning communities. When the environment is emotionally safe, when it is one that nurtures the students toward confident risk taking, you'll see kids who are comfortable with themselves and with each other.

Now one concrete way of creating this, is by being consistent. Something all individuals and all groups need for success. For consistency creates one mindset for all. And the starting point for this is through common language. Common language demonstrates the guiding principles of a class or a school. And in so doing, it tends to diffuse potentially volatile situations. It's less emotional. It's logical.

Teaching Empathy Institute

Appendix

It's predictable. When a cohort of teachers has a greater awareness of the significance of common language, new possibilities are manifested.

Reflection is the norm.

Now when a teacher is in the mode of self-reflection, the infusion ideas will flow, teachable moments will show up, moments built off of compassion for all. You can formalize these moments by telling your students that each day we create a legacy. Give it a name – the Wisdom Legacy Project. And implement it at the end of each day by asking a simple reflection question of your students. Something like: "what is one act of kindness that you practiced today?" And if you did this every day, by ritualizing this practice, you are saying "this is important". If you do this over and over again as a ritual, as an expected consistent practice, over time the question becomes an internal dialogue the child has, one which can take place anywhere, at any time.

I once heard of a study done in India which highlighted how, when people have what they called in the study "Portable God's," things they could bring with them away from the temple – to where they lived, to where they were with their family, to where they were working – when people could bring these portable gods with them, it gave them an inner strength. It created resilience. It was called the portability of strength. You don't have to be in a specific place to gain its value. You can take it wherever you go. So the simple practice of reflecting on kindness in the classroom during the school day can evolve into the practice of kindness outside of school. So the Wisdom Legacy Project is one simple strategy that can be implemented every day within your classroom.

Musical Interlude....

So here's a simple checklist of indicators of an emotionally safe learning community. This is what you will see. This is what sometimes they call "beginning with the end in mind." This is what we're looking toward. Students are helping one another, you hear supportive comments, there's a specific language that shows up. Sometimes people call this scripting. Now in pro-social skills training, or teaching, one of the steps that we take is we provide scripts for students. It's kind of like writing down your ideas before making a difficult phone call. Provide them with a script, let them practice it so they begin to internalize it, and now it's that internal dialogue once again. That language will show up.

We do this when we teach children how to say thank you. I know I'm a youth coach and there are some parents at the end of a practice, they'll always send their child up to thank me: "thanks, Coach," "thank you". And after a while the parent doesn't have to ask him to do it again. So, the child comes up to me: "thanks coach". And what do they get in return? A smile and appreciation back from me. They learn intuitively that by reaching out to others, they reach back in positive ways. That's relationship building and it comes from a simple act, a simple gesture, that starts with the script "go tell your coach 'Thank you'". Let me go through the first three again, and then I'll continue. There's two more. There's five total.

Here's the checklist:

- students are helping one another
- you hear supportive comments
- there's a specific language that shows up
- inclusion is the norm. Whether it's in the classroom, at specials, at lunch, at recess – everyone is involved, everyone is included. And part of inclusion is to allow someone the opportunity to be alone for a little bit. To include them, means to honor their needs and their feelings and sometimes they don't want to be a part of the group experience in that moment, on that day.
- The fifth one of the checklist: there are numerous opportunities for student recognition and celebration.

That's the simple checklist of indicators for an emotionally safe learning community.

You know I remember when I was growing up, when I was in school, the last thing I wanted was for my teacher to send a note home to my parents because it meant that I was going to be in trouble and that was going to be a rough night. So one simple celebratory practice to change the paradigm of this, is to send a note home that's a recognition report from time to time. Call it that: a recognition report.

Teaching Empathy Institute

Appendix

The recognition report trumpets the child's successes rather than identifying his or her issues, problems, or bad behaviors. By doing this, by sending a recognition report home from time to time, you absolutely cross over into the home and have influence over that child's experience for the rest of that afternoon and the rest of that evening.

So going back to Claudia's original quote from the start of the podcast – I'm going to add two words that relate to our work. I'm going to read her quote again with a slight addition: "Active consciousness is the capacity to observe, direct, and transform thoughts, emotions, and behaviors in order to manifest new possibilities" and joyful memories.

If simple practices can manifest new possibilities and joyful memories for our students, then I think you would agree that simple is not trivial, but rather deep, meaningful, and potentially life changing.